Adored

A Collection of Poetry
Volume II

By

HA Blackwood

Baying Hound Media

USA

Disclaimers and Copyright

This book is a work of fiction. Names, characters, places, and incidents are the product of the author's imagination and are used fictitiously. Any resemblance to actual persons, living or dead, locales, or events—no matter how much it seems like it's directed at you—is purely coincidental.

This book is protected under the copyright laws of the United States of America. Any reproduction or other unauthorized use of the material or artwork herein is prohibited under penalty of law without the express written permission of the author or publisher.

Adored

A Collection of Poetry
Volume II

Introduction

I've never considered myself to be a poet. If you've read the previous volume, I started this process with a specific purpose, but it's grown into something else. I've tapped into a part of my mind that I suppose has always been there (I did write an epic poem called "The Ballad Of The Bellyman" when I was 17) but has lain dormant for, well, decades.

I draw inspiration from the world around me. I see something - an image, or a word, or hear a line in a song - and I'm off and running. Sometimes a few lines will hit me while I'm in the shower (where most great ideas are formed, I find) or when I'm walking the dog and I grab my phone to record them before I forget them. Sometimes I wake from a dead sleep and the muse in my mind is screaming at me to jot some things down. I've found it's best to listen because the regret of a forgotten poem at six AM is a heavy burden indeed.

I enjoy the wordplay. The way the poems flow, the fitting together of lines and rhymes, or no rhymes, and deciding which to use and when. Each one is very much a puzzle to solve using infinite combinations of twenty-six letters, and I love that challenge. It's complex and sometimes agonizing and it's fun and so very worth it. Sometimes, when I try to write in one of my novels-in-progress and things aren't going well, I'll turn to poetry. I can't imagine NOT writing them now.

The process is so different from writing a novel. I can't really write a novel on the go on my phone. I've written many poems while walking. I can write a novel with or without music (though I prefer with) while poetry REQUIRES music – but only classical. It clears my mind and lets the words flow freely, but I can't have any lyrics in the music or it blocks my verbal chakras. Classical, however, wipes the slate of my mind clean, as it were.

Regardless of how, or why they exist, I hope you enjoy the next three hundred pages of poems. You'll see patterns – I go through phases where they're a little darker, or more erotic, or seasonal. Halloween and autumn in general are so rich for poetry. But enough jibber jabber. You grabbed this book for the poems, not to hear me wax rhapsodic about my process. What I really want to say is thank you for reading my work!

Hidden

There's music in you
That only I hear
Beautiful melodies
Just for my ears
There's beauty in you
That only I see
Hidden in plain view
But just meant for me
The love that we share
None can repeat
It's only for us
And makes us complete
All of my secrets
There are more than a few
Through the lens of that love
Are laid bare for you

Risen

My bones ache
And my spirit is weak
I may never find
The peace that I seek
Holes in my flesh
Wounds that won't heal
Scars under scars
This cannot be real
Angel of mercy
Take my hand
Show me the way
To your promised land
Down through the valley
Where the sinners they prey
Over the mountain
And cast me away
Adrift in the river
Out to the sea
Strip my bones bare
Til there's nothing of me
Only my essence
My patchwork soul
All that I am
All I control
Saltwater kisses
While sun bleaches bone
Yet through it all
I am not alone
The phoenix is risen
The man from the ash
Laid down before me
The long hidden path
I'll waste not a moment
The course it runs true
Each trial was worth it
For they led me to you

Enlightened

When there was a void
And day followed night
It was preordained
That you'd be my light
The one I'd be drawn to
In times low and high
That I'd give all my love to
Through the end of all time
Together forever
We greet each day
You're at my side, love
And that's where you'll stay
For just as it's fated
My light would be you
So will it be, love
I'll shine for you, too

Lucky Man

One lucky man
Gets to greet you each day
Calling you gorgeous
In myriad ways
One lucky man
Holds you at night
Tucking you in
And gripping you tight
One lucky man
Gets to love you out loud
To sing all your praises
And make you so proud
I've done something right
In a past life or three
For Fate to decide
That man should be me

Never

I never have to look
To see if you're with me
I know you're there
Just like I'd be
I never have to think
If this this love is real
We gave each other
What no one can steal
I never have to wonder
How long this will last
Forever's our future
Eternal's our past
I never have to doubt
What Fate has in store
For as much as she's given us
She has so much more
Wherever we go
Whatever we need
Happily bound
Together we'll be

Need to Feel

I feel
Warm in your arms
Held so tight
Protected from harm
I feel
Safe with your heart
Bathed in your love
Never shall part
I feel
Trusted with you
In all that we say
And all that we do
I feel
Loved all the time
The way that you
claimed me
And said "You are mine."
All of these things
And so many more
Wash over me
On our private shore
Your magic my love
Is patently real
You turn all my needs
Into things that I feel

Blessed

I gave you my heart
And you filled it with joy
I gave you my soul
And you stitched it to yours
I gave you my mind
And you built a world
Just for us
Secure, and safe
Warm, and loved
Where morning chats
And all day talks
And fun, dirty interludes
And trials and anxiety
And all of life's moments
Good and bad
High and low
Are handled together
Side by side
Trusting
Loving
Blessed
With you

Wonder

I'm lost in you
Your smile, your eyes
You pull me in
Make me your prize
Your goddess beauty
Your warrior's heart
You're full of magic
And oh so smart
I feel at ease
Inside your world
Safe and warm
My love unfurled
You're strong yet soft
And loving too
Is it any wonder
I'm lost in you?

Flawless

You're flawless, love
At least to me
Your skin is as perfect
As skin can be
Each freckle and scar
Stretch mark and mole
Are pieces of you
That make you whole
Each trial and setback
That stains your soul
Are part of the script
For playing your role
The battles you've fought
Those won and those lost
Are part of your being
And worth any cost
So you're flawless, love
At least to me
Each thing about you
Is as it should be

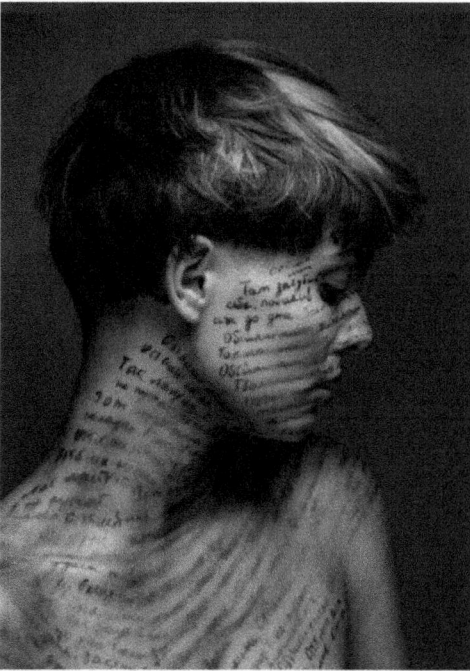

Lovers

There is a love affair
Between the moon and the sea
The moon pulls the sea closer
While it reflects her beauty
I am drawn to you
Like the sea to the moon
Your irresistible pull
Making me swoon
While your beauty I reflect
With my words so sweet
Shining your light
So the world can see
Fated lovers
The moon and the sea
Their story eternal
Like you and me

Fire

The fire in my heart
Burns out of control
Unlimited fuel
Igniting my soul
Consuming time
And burning a path
Forever is ours now
Destined to last
When we cast off our spark
You lit this fire
And laid all doubts
Upon the pyre
An ocean of flame
It's quite the view
But you're safe, my love
For I'm burning for you

Symbiosis

Like a river polishes stone
Over an eon or two
And water vapor rises
To turn the sky blue
Like the sun shines down
And makes flowers grow
And the bees buzz around
And make crops ready to sow
Like the moon pulls the tide
And surf crashes on land
Down through the ages
Creates a beach of soft sand
Like water and rock
Flowers and sun
When it comes to love
You are the one
Your soul has had mine
Under it's spell
Since the dawn of time
It's treated it well
Shaping our love
In all the right ways
So we'll fit together
For the rest of our days

Inevitable

Singular beauty
Incomparable mind
Kindness unmatched
Souls intertwined
Magical maiden
Down through time
Always for me
Her bell does chime
Hers from the start
My heart did belong
In every new life
It sings her song
I know that she'll find me
Fate makes it so
The closer we get
The brighter she'll glow
Made for each other
Her lock and my key
Opens a future
Where our love can run free

Callout

Across the darkness calls
Your soul to mine
I answer to the black
Across the void of time
I'll always have your back
As you have always had mine
Across the threshold creeps
Unwanted menacing slime
Together we shall keep
The threat across the line
I'll never leave your side
We'll rise above the grime
You place your hand in mine
Keeping me in thrall
And let your soul sing out
I'll always answer the call

Reflection

Drowning in the light
Of the midnight moon
Bodies pressed together
Fitting like two spoons
Hand pressed to hand
Naked in bliss
Knowing that forever
It will be like this
Soul wrapped in soul
Hearts beat as one
The moon glows so bright
Reflecting the sun
As day follows night
Skies turn black to blue
And my glow, my love
Is a reflection of you

Residence

Late at night
When the house is dark
And quiet reigns
And sleep is sparse
My mind is filled
With thoughts of you
Of your loving touch
And your eyes of blue
Your hand in mine
Fingers laced
Joined together
Heartbeats paced
We roam at will
Each other's mind
A more perfect fit
We'll never find
Connected through
Both space and time
We both reside
Inside this rhyme

Arrival

She came for me
From beyond the sky
This perfect woman
Inside my eye
She came for me
Across an ocean of time
She knew it when
Her soul touched mine
She came for me
With intention true
With a heart so pure
For our love's debut
She came for me
Her timing right
Her magnet's pull
Her beacon's light
A luckier man
There will never be
For I gave her my heart
When she came for me

Aligned

I loved you from the start
Though I didn't know then
And you warned me not to
I still gave you my heart
I loved you from the start
It couldn't be stopped
Our poles aligned
And never pulled apart
You loved me too
It was hard to admit
You tried to protect it
But your heart was true
You loved me too
And you soon found
You'd never known love
Like I have for you
We were meant to be
Each other's true north
Matched by Fate
A lock and her key
We were meant to be
It's plain to us now
I was made to love you
And you are perfect for me

Sensations

Lightning in the sky
Thunder on the ground
Beauty in my eye
Loving all around
Wind across my skin
Rain upon my face
Glowing from within
Wrapping me in grace
Sun breaks through the clouds
And shines upon the earth
Your beauty sings aloud
Our souls have given birth
A love so strong and new
Never shall it fail
We're one instead of two
On the sea of love we sail
The moon shines at night
The stars they bid us roam
Wherever you're in sight
That is now my home

Glowing

The glow that I see
When you look at me
Is the beauty inside
You no longer hide
You light up the room
Push back the gloom
Show the whole world
Your beauty unfurled
It comes from down deep
Where your secrets you keep
I've always known
How brightly you glow
Our love has awoke
From the moment we spoke
That we're meant to be
Was obvious to me
And clearly it too
Was obvious to you
For the glow that I see
You've always shown me

Until

Time has no meaning
Since I met you
An hour, a day
Burned away
You're all I see
When I close my eyes
Hopes and dreams
And impossible things
All I feel is you
Connected
Heart, brain, and soul
Love continues to grow
All that I am
All that I know
Led to this
Emotional bliss
Before we met
I did only exist
I wanted to thrive
But I'd never been alive
Until I met you

Potential

Spoken words
Yet to be sung
Pealing bell
Yet to be rung
Rising Sun
In the darkened sky
Soaring eagles
Who've yet to fly
A life time of love
I've yet to give
A storybook ending
We've yet to live
So many things
Have yet to be
Written in the stars
For you and me

Wanted

My head swims
With thoughts of you
Easy to love
And brilliant too
Filled with talent
And a soul so strong
We were meant to be
All along
Galactic eyes
And a body that kills
Physical perfection
Wanton thrills
Endless nights
With fun galore
Beautiful days
That I adore
No matter what
We say or do
Forever I want
To do it with you

Addition

Fresh sheets
Against our skin
So good for sleeping
Even better for sin
The smell of coffee
Fresh morning brew
Caffeine and kisses
Just for you
Flowers and candy
Beauty and sweet
You are my lover
I am your treat
Each little moment
Means so much
Pleasing our senses
Enhancing our touch
I pay attention
Whatever we do
For all of the small things
Add up to you

Through

Through my eyes
There's a glow
Coming from your soul
Through my eyes
Your beauty shines
Like nothing before
Through my eyes
You are perfect
This you know
For through my eyes
I always show you
How I see
Through my eyes
I have visions
Of what will be
Through my eyes
We are Fated
Through and through
Through my eyes
It is always
Me and you

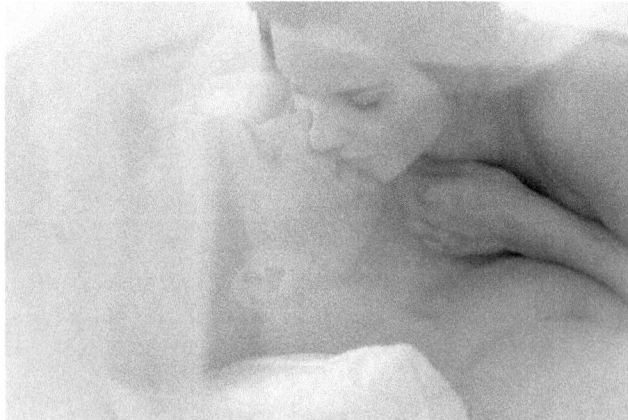

Spirits

I feel your breath
Upon my skin
Are we sleeping
Or engaged in sin
I hold you tight
I need you so
Now you're mine
I won't let go
You cling to me
Your need the same
Your hands grip tight
You say my name
Our love is pure
Our spirits soar
Together now
And evermore

Craving

Late in the night
Thoughts of you fill my head
Why are you there
Not in my bed
Why am I here
And not in your arms
How can I keep you
From coming to harm
Connected in mind
Wrapped in your soul
Craving your body
Wanting you whole
We fit each other
When push comes to shove
Distance is nothing
Compared to our love

Vision

I see you in the summer sky
Bright with sun
Or storm's damp eye
I see you in the flowery field
Bright with colors
That never yield
I see you when my eyes are closed
Brightly glowing
Flowing prose
I see you in my life infused
Brightening all
With the love I choose
You're everywhere
In everything
My heart is full
My soul it sings
I hope your eyes
Of gleaming blue
Everywhere
Can see me too

Timebound

I've looked for you a thousand times
In a thousand lands
In a thousand lives
Every time the hand of Fate
Picked the time
We'd meet as mates
My perfect love
Your happy man
Blessed from above
In every life
We've made it through
The toil and strife
Sometimes it's rough
The time we have
Is not enough
But I would live
A hundred years
If Fate would give
Just one day
For us two
And I could say
I love you

Resting

We lay down to get some rest
Either as spoons
Or with your head on my chest
I don't know which one I like best
When we're in spoons
We touch head to toe
My arms wrapped around you
And our souls' warming glow
But head on chest
Feels so great
Your body on mine
Loving your weight
My heart beats for you
Right in your ear
I hold you so tight
And love you so dear
They both feel so good
How can I choose?
They are both perfectly suited
For our nighttime snooze
And to make it more tough
To choose the best way
You throw a curve
And perfect our day
You're my big spoon
Gripping me tight
Keeping me safe
All through the night
It's so hard to pick
But I'll tell you what's true
My favorite nights
Are those spent with you

Truth

Never have I known
A love so true
As that which I feel
When I look at you
Your eyes penetrate
And pierce my soul
Your mind grabs me
And takes control
Your fingers grip mine
And never let go
That you'd fit me so well
Only Fate could know
I see you each day
Everywhere I look
You flow through my veins
Like a fiery brook
You're my alpha and omega
My first thought and last
My unending future
My beautiful past
Never have I known
A love so true
And I'm eternally grateful
I get to love you

Cliches

Cute as a button
Free as a breeze
These are cliches
That could apply to me
Sharp as a tack
Hot as the sun
Are a couple that I
Could apply to you for fun
Soft as a cloud
Smart as a whip
Pretty as a picture
All come from the hip
There are hundreds of ways
To complement you
And I'll spend my life
Seeing that through
But for now let me say
There's not enough glue
To adequately describe
How I'm stuck on you

Natural Beauty

Hair that cascades like a waterfall
A voice smooth like a petal from a pink rose
Eyes that blaze like blue fire
A spirit like the universe perpetually grows
I see nature's beauty in you
And in you I see nature's glow
You're woven into my fabric
And stitched into my soul
I carry you in my heart
And take you wherever I go

Summertime

Summer skies
Of brilliant blue
And endless things
For us to do
Barbecues
And games to play
Loving smiles
That last for days
The fireflies
That dot the night
The starry skies
Which fill our sight
Soon enough
I'll be ready for fall
But while summer's here
I want it all
The sunny fun
The clothing thin
The thunderstorms
That soak our skin
Holding hands
Kissing lips
Smiling eyes
Dancing hips
Summer skies
Of brilliant blue
And summer nights
Spent with you

Safe Space

A soft touch
A gentle embrace
A brush of lips
A hand on my face
A whispered need
A moaning plea
Tells me exactly
What you need from me
A grasping hand
A writhing hip
Shouting desire
Tightening your grip
Flowing current
Skin to skin
Pulling me close
Drawing me in
Ever we're lovers
A safe space to be
Our sanctuary
Is in you and me

Travelers

Across space and time
I traveled here
When I was but a soul
Searching for love so dear
The moment we met
So long in the past
We knew it was meant
Forever to last
Across the ages
Together as one
No matter the trial
We'll not be undone
We've faced every danger
And triumphed through all
It's not always easy
But we always stand tall
In each life I find you
At just the right time
With help from Fate
I make you mine
What she doesn't tell me
Is that you're so well versed
That by the time we meet
You've claimed me first

Stolen Moments

Morning sun dances
Off your blissful face
Coffee in your hands
Happy in your space
Quiet moments
Meant to enjoy
Watching you
I play it coy
A feast for my eyes
I drink you in
My perfect love
My soul's sweet twin
I could watch you there
All day long
Stealing my breath
My heart in song
But you catch a glimpse
With your eyes of blue
And pat the seat
Next to you
I snuggle up
And squeeze you tight
You squeeze me back
With all your might
"It's a lovely day"
As I kiss your brow
You touch my cheek
"It's perfect now"

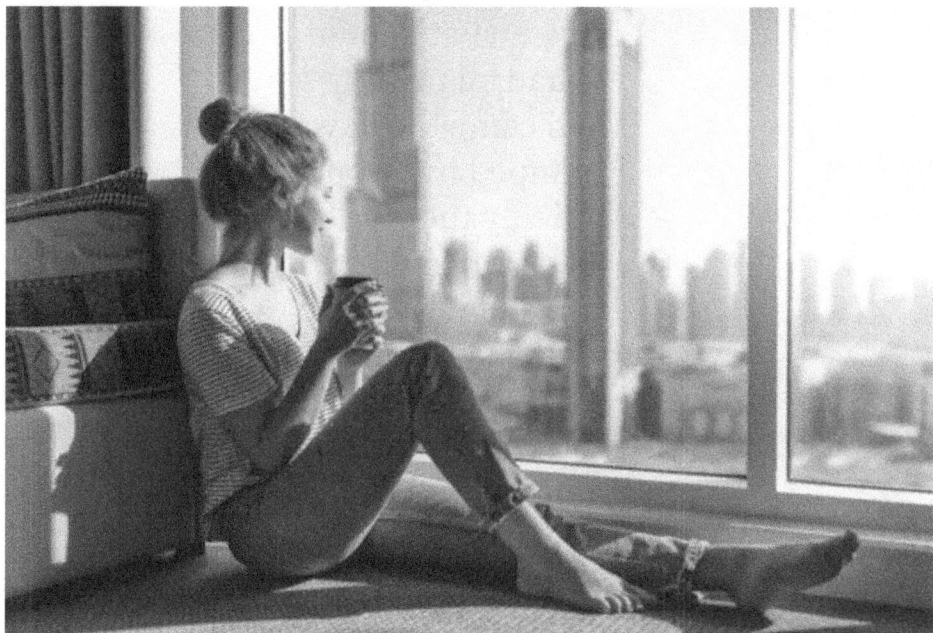

Refreshed

There was a time
I thought my race was run
I'd seen what I could
I'd had all my fun
Then came the day
I bumped into you
Suddenly the world
Was bright and new
I gained new purpose
And filled up with hope
You showed me fresh life
At the end of my rope
And your life was changed
In a similar way
When our magnets clicked
On that Fate driven day
You saw your world
Through a new set of eyes
Ones that adored you
And saw your soul rise
A love everlasting
From the dawn of time
Marked down forever
In rhyme after rhyme

Reactions

I like the way it feels
When you're on my mind
The signals that brain sends out
My body responds in kind
My heart it pounds inside my chest
My skin it gets so flush
My breath is stolen in a gasp
It's a total endorphin rush
No matter how many times I see
Your face, or just your name
The butterflies kick up a fuss
I'll never be the same
I hope you feel the same things, love
It really is quite fun
To react this way time and again
And know you are the one

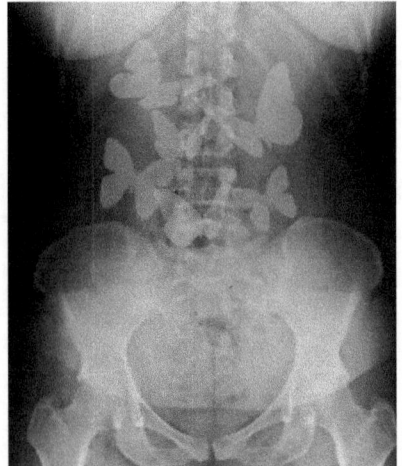

Transcends

Like the pealing thunder
My heart beats for you
Like the rising sun
I see you each day anew
Like the nighttime sky
You dazzle my eyes
Like my perfect lover
I respond to your cries
Like my best friend
I can count on you
Like a resurrection stone
You make me feel brand new
Wherever I go
Whatever I do
You're part of me now
As I'm part of you
Together in spirit
And also in mind
Ours is a love
That transcends space and time

Summer loving

Lush green fields
And billowing trees
Hand holding hand
Was made for days like these
Hot summer sun
Drinks in the shade
Sweet knowing looks
Of which my dreams are made
Fireflies
Short sun dress
Tanned thighs
Things I like best
But the best part of summer
And the other seasons too
Is every day
I get to spend with you

Nighttime

You're far away
In the dead of night
I wake with a start
Something's not right
Whether you just can't sleep
Or aren't feeling well
The signal is vague
It's hard to tell
One thing I know
It doesn't deceive
When I get this feeling
I must believe
So I'll send my thoughts
And energy to you
And know that Fate
Will get it through
Our hearts are connected
And covered in stardust
And in our fated love
I'll always place my trust

Our World

If the sun stopped its shine
I would be okay
I get the light I need
When I look at your face
If the moon stopped its glow
I would be alright
I get the tide pull I need
Snuggled with you at night
If the rain ceased its fall
I would make it through
No drought can claim me
When I'm with you
The world we've made
Through which we run
Is impervious to harm
And can't come undone
All that I feel
All that I see
Is perfect, my love
With you next to me

With You

The sky could cave In
Never again show blue
And I would don't care
As long as I'm with you
The ground could quake
And swallow us too
And I wouldn't care
As long as I'm with you
The big bad wolf could show up
And huff and puff right on cue
It won't matter a whit to me
As long as I'm with you
No matter the tribulation
Or trial we face
Nothing can stop us
Or damage our grace
So the world can try
And do what it will do
And none of it matters
As long as I'm with you

You are

You are a hit song
That never grows old
A four course meal
That never gets cold
A favorite movie
I can watch any time
An unending poem
With unending rhymes
You're my sunshine
My crescent moon
My perfect angel
Who makes me swoon
The safe arms
I crawl into at night
The warrior goddess
At whose side I'll fight
My morning coffee
My afternoon tea
The be-all end-all
You're it for me

Seen

I see in you a magic
No one else can see
A power like no other
A power over me
I see in you a light
Too bright for most to see
Illuminates your soul
Burning bright and free
I see in you a passion
Few are blessed to see
For life and love and knowledge
And I am drawn to thee
For I see in you the future
Where you and I are found
The hand of Fate decided
That together we'd be bound
I see in you a thousand things
And each day a thousand more
Ever will we be in love
Always will our spirits soar

Night Moves

In my mind
I hold you tight
Loving you
As we say goodnight
Our energy
Affects the world
Warm winds blow
Flags unfurl
Outside my window
Through the screen
The sky opens up
Washes us clean
The very moment
We start to doze
Rain comes down
And restores our souls
In my mind
I hold you tight
Together, love
We rule the night

Piece By Piece

I just stare at your picture
And feel my heart leaving
Piece by piece
Until it lands
Safely
In your hands
I told you once
I would give you the world
Piece by piece
Starting with my heart
Staring at your beauty
Frozen in time
Is how it had to start

Fluent

We have a language all our own
We each understand the other
By what's not said
As much as what is
And the magic of it is
We never have to try
We're fluent with our bodies
With our minds
And with our hearts

Shooting Star

Out of all the stars
That have fallen from the sky
It's a miracle of Fate
That you are mine
I made a wish,
Plucked a lash
Counted three
And thanked the gods
And Fate alike
That they sent you here
To be with me

Magic Moments

Our magic can't be held
By the walls in which we live
It seeps into the world
Like water through a sieve
It makes the flowers bloom
In all our favorite shades
It brings the late day rains
As the sunlight starts to fade
It makes the crickets sing
In time to my beating heart
It brings my love to you
The bullseye for my dart
It makes the moon shine bright
And the stars glow just for you
It links our minds on a higher plane
There's not much it can't do
Of all the things our magic does
Of all that feel so right
The one I like the very most
Is holding you all night

Cause and Effect

You're first on my mind
No matter when I wake
Midnight, two, or break of dawn
My breath is always yours to take
The last thought every night
Is always some version of you
How you affect the world at large
Blooms of lilac shining through
I hold you tight through the dark
And lift you up into the light
Your soul glows from deep within
Electrifying me at your sight
You never know the effect you have
When you turn your eyes to me
My fiery blood, my stolen breath
Your smiling face sets me free

HA Blackwood

Forever Bound

She is my moon
I take her in and hold her
Waxing, full, and waning
As though I'm breathing her in and out
For one moment empty, missing her
Before she fills me again
I am the sea
My tide surrounds her
She rises and falls with me
As though she's riding me like a wave
For one minute, ebbed, missing me
Before rising again
Both filled with the other
Forever bound
Eternal in love

Bonded

My hand on your cheek
Lips on your neck
Body on fire
Desire unchecked
Your hand in my hair
Watermelon lips
Desperate cries
Grinding of hips
Like a match strikes its cover
Our passions ablaze
Need takes over
Brain in a daze
Hand on your neck
My lips on your cheek
Craving so strong
It hits fevered peak
All that we want
All that we see
Is found in the bond
Between you and me

One Thing

What in the world would I do
To keep your heart with me so true
I'd swim across the ocean blue
If it kept me next to you
I'd climb the highest peak around
Or dig the deepest hole in the ground
I'd race around the world twice
Just to keep our souls so bound
I'd fight an army all alone
And explore all parts unknown
To keep your love next to me
I would map all earth and sea
As luck would have it
For you and me
None of that is necessary
For our love was set by Fate
We walked our miles
And paid our freight
And so to keep your love by me
There's just one thing that I must do
And that's unconditionally keep loving you

Days Gone

There was a time before we met
But I really don't remember it
It seems my life began anew
The day I began knowing you
The day we felt the magnets click
Was when Fate pulled her clever trick
I didn't know then I'd fall for you
And never thought you'd love me too
But Fate was sure of her plan's success
Eternal happiness and nothing less
There was a time before we met
But I really don't remember it
And really, why would I want to
When I have a future filled with you

One Thousand

A thousand times you've called my name
Floating out upon the night
A thousand times I've heard your call
My voice in your ear feeling right
A thousand times you've come for me
In circumstances great and small
A thousand times I've held you tight
A better fit I can't recall
A thousand times we've felt the pull
Of aligning magnetic poles
A thousand times we've met in space
Wrapped inside our magic souls
A thousand times we've given all
To make each other's dreams come true
As for the next thousand lives
I'm giving every one to you

Long Distance

Even though we've never met
I can taste you on me yet
My fingers have never touched your skin
But they're dripping with our sin
My neck has never felt your breath
But that sensation I love to death
You've never run your fingers through my hair
But I swear that I can feel them there
I've never had my hand on the small of your back
But the way I tingle you can't convince me of that
So let's dream all our dreams
And fantasize too
And ignite this connection
Between me and you

Love Songs

All you need is love
The Beatles famously sang
And it's oft repeated
So close to home it rang
Stevie Ray Vaughan was Love Struck Baby
Van Halen said Love Walks In
Sammy Hagar said he Don't Need Love
But he'll Fall In Love Again
Love Her Madly advise The Doors
And Love Her Two Times as well
Social D in When She Begins
Says that woman put them under a spell
The Cure wrote a tune called Love Song
Lana Del Rey and Tesla did too
But I think U2 said it best
When it comes to our love, All I Need Is You

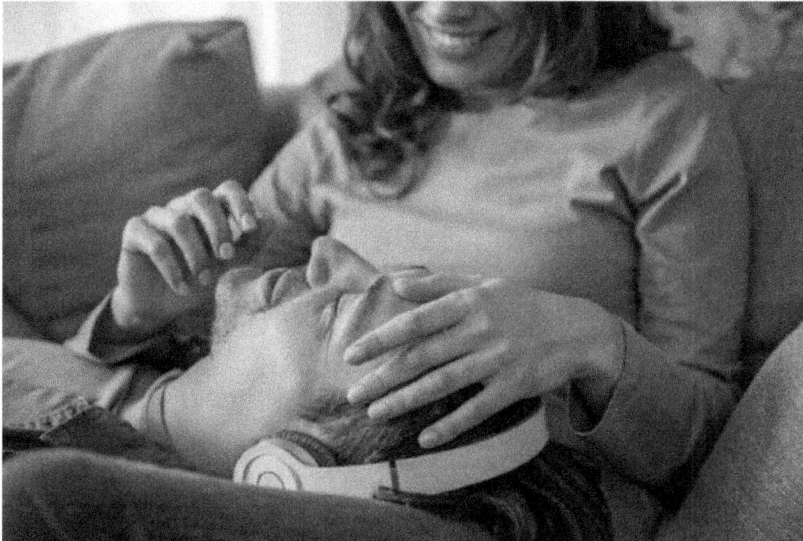

All Things

You're a lifeline
On a sea tempest-tossed
You're the future
I once thought was lost
You're a beacon
Shining in the sky
You're the reason
I never wonder why
You're the rocket booster
That takes me to space
You're my racing heart
When I see your face
You're my morning sun
My evening moon
My midday rain
My midnight swoon
My beautiful day
My lovely night
My little spoon
When I hold you tight
You're an angel's wings
A magicians dove
My perfect fit
My fated love

Warrior Souls

There's nothing that can keep me from you
No villain strong enough to take me down
Nothing that the universe can do
No obstacle I can't get around
No matter what may yet unfold
The thread of Fate has no slack
As far as I may get thrown
To you I'll find my way back
I know you're as tough as they get
And battle tested as you are
You're quick to have your sword in hand
And find me whether near or far
Our hearts they beat together now
Our souls are stitched together too
You've got my back and I've got yours
There's nothing that can keep me from you

Beyond Compare

I'll never find words enough
To tell you how I feel
To adequately describe to you
The depth of your appeal
To what do I compare you
When you're beyond compare?
How do I convey these feelings
That are impossible to share?
You can't feel my butterflies
As they flip and flutter inside
You can't feel the electricity
As it zips along my hide
You don't feel the gasp
Of every breath you steal
You don't feel the racing pulse
That my flushed skin reveals
I'll just have to find a way
To get your mind to see
With every word that I can find
How much you mean to me

Eternal Love

How lucky am I to live right now
When I have been matched
To you somehow
Fate has smiled and cast her spell
We made our choices
And then we fell
Nothing else can feel like this
No siren's call
Can stop this bliss
My one true love, my fated mate
Half a lifetime
We had to wait
Our life together stretches ahead
Bound together
By the strongest thread
Eternal love you give to me
And by your side
I'll always be
My queen, my goddess, my love so true
All my lives
I give to you

Complementary

Stardust and moonlight
Dance upon my skin
Your elemental magic
Working its way in
Fingertips and kisses
Placed upon my chest
Lips as soft as roses
Surely I am blessed
Arms that wrap around you
Pulling you so tight
Ocean's tide rolling
Feeling all my might
Complementary powers
Combining our delight
Our days they are amazing
But pale next to our nights
We're meant to be together
The gods and Fate agree
Bound each to the other
Glowing moon and shining sea

Faith

What would you do
A question I often ask
I trust your intuition
When faced with a difficult task
You're steeped in quiet wisdom
You earned it through your life
You've learned a thousand lessons
From every struggle and strife
So when I have cause to wonder
Exactly what to do
I close my eyes and visualize
And take my cues from you
You're my perfect partner
We're matched in every way
Where I have a weakness
Your strengths come into play
So when I need some guidance
And I don't have a clue
I close my eyes and visualize
And put my faith in you

Pledged

You're always on my mind
Awake, you're all I see
Even when I'm sleeping
You occupy my dreams
I miss you when we part
The second that we leave
But fonder grows my heart
My love knows no reprieve
Upon delightful return
I instantly rejoice
I'll never get enough
Of your face, your touch, your voice
There's magic in our love
You'll certainly agree
We've pledged both heart and soul
In choices Fated and free
That means when we're distant
And each other we pursue
I keep you in my heart, my love
As you keep me there with you

I See You

I see you as an angel
Sent from heaven up above
Forget the wings and halo
You came to me with love
I see you as a goddess
Beautiful and pure
On earth there there is no equal
Of that I am quite sure
I see you as a warrior
Strong and unafraid
There's nothing that can beat you
Your courage on display
I see you as my lover
Sexy as can be
Confident in your body
And what you do to me
I see you as a partner
Supportive on demand
I can always count on you
Walking hand in hand
Of all the ways I see you
Of all the images I send
First and foremost, love
You'll always be my friend

Force of Nature

There's nothing in the world
That can keep me from you
The planet can churn
And chaos ensue
A class five hurricane
Or a tornado can blow
A blizzard can sweep in
With six feet of snow
The earth can quake
And mud can slide
Rain can pour down
And rivers can rise
None of it matters
Regarding you and me
My faith's in Fate
Because we're meant to be
So no matter the season
Or what nature can brew
There's nothing in the world
That can keep me from you

All I Am

Up in the heavens
Out on the sea
In the depths of space
You're always with me
Sleeping in our bed
Wrapped up in my arms
Giving all your love
Receiving all your charms
Running through my mind
Part of every thought
I always feel your presence
The thread of Fate so taut
Every morning starts with you
Just as every evening ends
Every smile has your spark
And the joy it sends
Everything I am, my love
Everything you see
Contains a piece of you inside
For you're everything to me

Rarest Love

Never before and never again
Has there been a love like ours
I'm sure lots of people feel that way
But we've been picked by the stars
We each walked a path alone
Not knowing we would meet
The choices made have led us here
No other souls could compete
Our poles aligned and magnets clicked
And two became as one
Our ragged edges perfectly matched
We'll never come undone
The magic that has brought us here
Is beautiful to behold
Fate presented a chance to us
And we both grabbed ahold
From now until the end of time
Our love will burn so bright
Through twenty five thousand perfect days
And just as many nights
Never will our desire flag
Or our passions wane
For never has there been a love like ours
And there never will again

Effective

I love it when you catch me
When I'm unaware
With your words, your image
Whatever you share
The way my heart beats
My pulse like thunder
The gasp in my breath
Eyes wide with wonder
The way your glow
Lights up the land
Ferocious and bright
But warm in my hand
The music in your laugh
The song of your voice
Igniting my blood
How I rejoice
Your magical smile
Gives me such life
I am eternal
Free of all strife
You know the effect
You have on me
And I look forward to feeling it
For eternity

Seat of Power

I could have lived
Ten thousand years
Traveled the earth
Faced all my fears
Won every trial
I'd ever faced
Found every foe
And laid them to waste
Climbed every mountain
Swam every sea
None of it would matter
Without you next to me
I could command an army
And conquer the world
And what would I profit
If you weren't my girl
I could rule from on high
All I could view
It all would be worthless
If I didn't have you
To be truly wealthy
There's one thing I need
Not lust for power
Or overwhelming greed
I don't need a scepter
Or piles of gold
I just need you beside me
As I grow old

Destiny Revealed

Long ago and far away
Our Fate was sealed
Each life we'd walk alone
Until our destiny revealed
A warrior goddess
None can compare
My soul ever seeking
Enemies beware
Times they change
But our love never will
We'll face any challenge
And climb any hill
It never matters
What times we see
I'll find you my love
Just as you'll find me

Belonging

You belong
In my arms each morning
I belong
Right next to you
You belong
Where the moon is shining
I belong
Where you're my only view
We belong
Together on this adventure
We belong
Where the trail is fun and new
We belong
Where we can dance under lightning
We belong
With this love so strong and true

Take Me

Take me to the sky
You said with your eyes
We'll touch the moon
And make it our prize
Take me to the sea
I said with my heart
The moon makes the tide
The two cannot part
Take me to your heart
You said with your soul
I promise to love it
And keep it whole
Wrap me in your soul
I said with mine
I promise to love you
Across space and time
You placed a kiss
Upon my mouth
And said to me
I'll make you this vow
I'll give you my soul
My heart and my time
We'll share this love
As I make you mine

Gifted

The sun rises and I see your glow
The morning dew heavy in the air
You are my source of strength
I feel your presence everywhere
The wind blows and I hear your voice
A whisper of you surrounding me
Heaven sent for my ears alone
Magical, musical, and so carefree
The rain falls and I feel your touch
Soft and delicate on my skin
Making my nerves tingle and sing
Lighting my fire from within
I know you experience similar things
When you look to the heavens above
Everywhere you look and touch
You find reminders of our love
Nature is filled with pieces of us
Earthly wisps and celestial taunts
Even apart we're never alone
For the gods know our needs and wants
So next to me or across the land
We never feel our love abate
Always there, our hearts display
A gift to us from the hand of Fate

Golden

A never ending flood of emotion
A perpetual smile on my face
A love for which I'd swim the ocean
A beauty that crosses time and space
A moment when a choice was made
A plan long known was set in motion
A fated pair's connection date
A thousand lives of pure devotion
When poles aligned the world changed
Never had we had this notion
We never knew it could be so good
Ever grateful for this plan's promotion
Years from now, when stories told
This will be the first in line
Showing how trusting fate
Leads to something so sublime
A choice, a path, a plan, two hearts
Elements of our tale told
We had the chance and made the most
And now our love has turned to gold

Fairy Tale

Once upon a morning's rise
Was a woman with eyes of blue
I wasn't searching yet there you were
I never dreamed it would be you
When the morning came and went
Was a man's eyes filled with glee
You weren't searching yet there I was
You couldn't know it was meant to be
Unexpected as it was
Day by day we both could tell
Matched by Fate were our souls
With smiling eyes we both fell
Years from now, our story told
When our road is finally done
We'll see each other with wizened eyes
Forever grateful we found the one
Fairy tales do come true
Though not with eyes of damsel nor prince
We just let go of doubt and fear
And lived in love ever since

Phrasing

Down in the dumps
Up in the air
Slogans and cliches
Are everywhere
Shit happens
It's understood
But then you remember
That life is good
Every saying
Has a grain of truth
Just don't lament
Your misspent youth
You might think
And I don't blame you if you do
That my favorite phrase
Is I love you
But there's one more
At this point in time
That's close to my heart
You are mine.

Being You

You don't know the effect you have
Just by being you
The things that you unlock in me
With all you say and do
The smiles that you bring
Upon this happy face
The way your eyes take me
On a trip through outer space
Quick witted answers
That keep me on my toes
Thoughtful broad discussions
And sharing what you know
The ease with which you bring me
To a different point of view
You make me a better person
Just by being you

All Together

When your demons rise
And your way is lost
I will have your back
No matter the cost
When our skies are gray
And rain does fall
Never fear my love
I'm here through it all
We're together now
As we've always been
We've seen tough times
And we will again
The important thing
To keep in mind
You're never alone
We're two of a kind
I'm never afraid
Of what may come
For you're at my side
And will never run
We're together now
As we'll always be
I'm here for you
And you've got me

Binding

Promises are everywhere
When you look around
Explicit or implied
Promises abound
The promise of a new day
It's always understood
Gives us hope anew
The next one could be good
A promissory note
Should be ironclad
But we learned when the bubble burst
Some promises go bad
When it comes to you and I
And the promises we make
We know they're from our souls
Impossible to fake
A promise is a contract
Binding if you're true
And here's one that I'll make, love
I'll always stand by you

Gifted Hearts

Your tender heart felt just right
The second that you gave it to me
Taking that great leap of faith
Not yet knowing we were meant to be
As scary as this was to start
There was no way for you to know
When it came to gifting hearts
I'd given you mine some time ago
I gave it before I knew I did
We were such a perfect fit
And so naturally did we flow
I never thought to question it
Once we both came tumbling down
We knew that we had got it right
We have such fun through every day
And love and laugh through every night
From now until the end of time
We'll hold hands and beam with pride
For nowhere would we rather be
Than here together, side by side

Would You Rather

I'd rather fall a hundred feet
And go splat upon the ground
Than miss one moment with you, love
And this magic that we've found
I'd rather take a million volts
Directly to my derrière
Than miss a kiss from your lips
While running my fingers through your hair
An ACME rocket off a cliff
Would be a preferable choice
If the alternate option was
Never again hearing your voice
If I were told my days were done
And nevermore would I touch your skin
I'd fight Mike Tyson in his prime
If we got to start again
I can think of a thousand things
That I would rather suffer through
Than spend a single moment here
Where I wasn't loving you

Into Forever

I don't remember
Before there was you
What love was like
Or how I knew
Before there was you
Did I ever smile?
Was I happy?
Was life worthwhile?
It doesn't matter
In the end
The past is past
I comprehend
The present's gift
Is time with you
The future's promise
We'll make anew
Hand in hand
We're meant to be
Into forever
It's you and me

Nature's Fury

Wind can howl and storms can rage
And still I'm there with you
Nature's fury can try its best
But can't separate we two
If mankind fell and zombies rose
A plague of biblical size
I'd find a way to get to you
Despite the undead rise
Killer bees and fire ants
And spiders that can fly
None of them can keep me away
No matter how they try
So when the heavens shake
And the thunder roars
And the ground does quake
And the raindrops pour
Know that I will be there
Standing at your door
Nothing keeps we two apart
In love forevermore

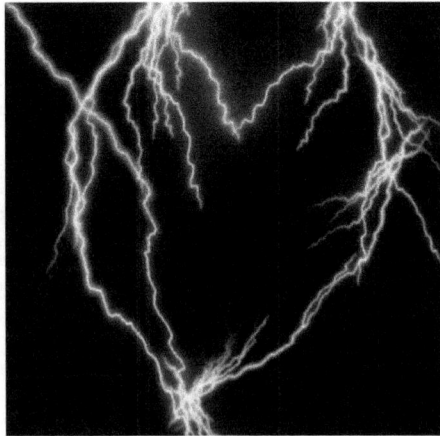

Automatic

I breathe because I must
Without oxygen I will die
Breathing is automatic
And we never wonder why
My heart's on autopilot
Never taking a moments rest
Pushing fire through my veins
As it beats within my chest
And so it is with loving you
It's a natural part of me
There's never any question
About our love's decree
I say I'll always choose you
In a loud and steady voice
But like breathing or my beating heart
It's never been a choice
My love is automatic
Unconditional and true
The moment that our souls connected
My love belonged to you

Masterpiece

A smile like a ray of sun
Aimed straight at my heart
A voice like a symphony
Each word a work of art
Iridescent eyes
Lure like a siren's song
Falling under your spell
Could never feel wrong
Your image is a masterpiece
No artist could create
Carved with love by the hands of gods
There's really no debate
As perfect as you are to me
It wouldn't mean a thing
If it wasn't for your mind
And the wonders that it brings
Before you say a word
About issues you perceive
Know each imperfection
Makes you beautifully unique
So when you look into the mirror
I'll tell you what you see
An uncompromising beauty
Who's exactly what I need

Safe Haven

You lit my blood on fire
And broke me from my chains
I'll burn for you forever
With fire in my veins
You are my magic stardust
You are my midnight sun
You are my soul's safe haven
So to your arms I run
Always will we keep each other
Safe and happy and warm
No matter what may come our way
We'll weather any storm
You know I crave your presence
Your soul, your body and mind
And always will I burn for you
From now through the end of time

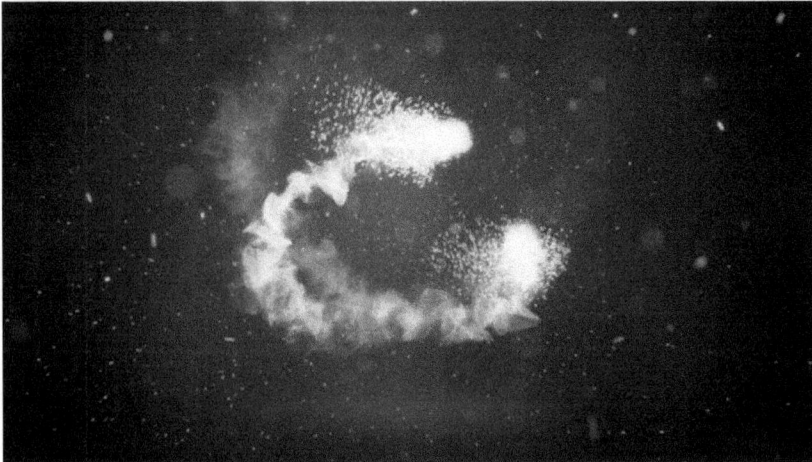

Feel Like I Do

I hope you can feel
The things I do
The wants and needs
The physical pull
The butterflies
And pulse's rise
The longing ache
Between my thighs
The relief of hearing
Your voice's tone
The way you're here
Even when I'm alone
Our love is magic
And perfectly tuned
And baby I know
You feel it too

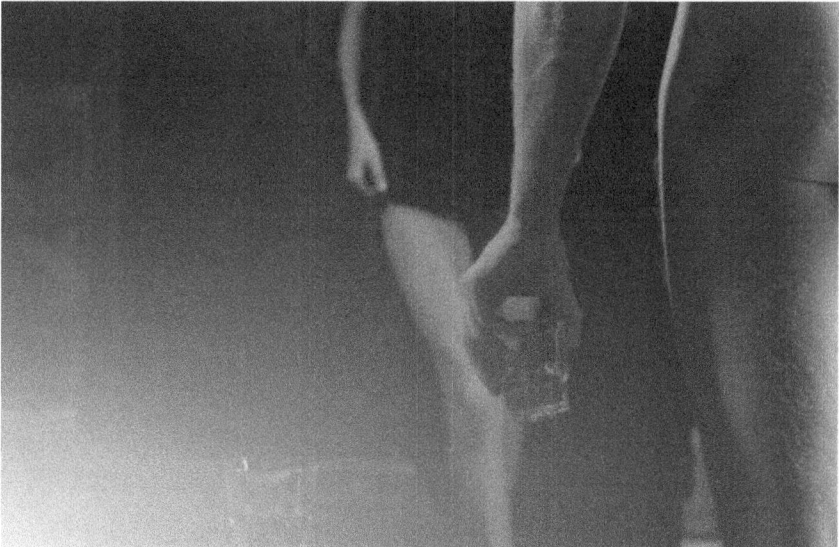

One Day

One day you'll know
What it's like to see you
Through these eyes
What it it's like to feel you
In this heart
What it's like to know you
In this mind
What it's like to claim you as mine
And love you
Without conditions
One day I'll know
How you see me
Feel me
Know me
Own me
And love me
Without conditions
And we'll find it feels the same
For we're two halves of our whole
Perfectly matched
Edges aligned
Wrapped in each other
Til the end of time

I Wish

I wish I had all the answers
And knew the right things to say
I wish I could grab the bad things
And throw them all away
I wish I could protect you
And everyone you love
From all the types of harm
That can befall them from above
It's not within my power
No matter how I wish
It hurts to feel so helpless
Especially in times like this
But I can be here for you
And hold you oh so tight
So you know that you're not alone
On even the darkest night
It may not make things better
As if they were never bad
But if it helps a little bit
I'll be so very glad
I don't have a superpower
Bestowed from gods above
But I'll make use of what I've got
And give you all my love

Your Moonlight

Bathe me in your moonlight
Let me drink you from my cup
Bestow on me your warm sweet glow
And fill my soul with love
Take me so completely
My body, soul, and mind
Explore with me new worlds
As we travel space and time
Take me on adventures
Wherever we may roam
It matters not where we go
For in your heart I'm home
Bathe me in your moonlight
Pull me to your shore
Fill me with desire
And love me evermore

Love Is

Love is such a simple word
Yet it means a lot of things
When it's right like it is with us
There's a universe it brings
I love you strong and fiercely
I love you because you're you
I love your soul completely
And forever I'll be true
You love me with devotion
You love me through and through
You love me so uniquely
That I'll always belong to you
Loving you is easy
For we are meant to be
It's as natural as breathing
Or as you loving me
Until the day I die
I'll be in a state of bliss
For I have been allowed to feel
Such a love as this

Dawn Of Time

We stared across forever
And sailed oceans of time
To finally be together
In body, spirit and mind
Across the vastness of space
Our souls did travel entwined
To have you lay your claim on me
And make you likewise mine
A hundred thousand lifetimes
Have led to here and now
And a hundred thousand more
Won't be enough somehow
For I'll never get my fill of you
Regardless of the time
I'll always have more love to give
And always have more rhymes
From the universe's dawn
We were meant to be
And until the cosmos dies
It will always be you and me

Syllables

Every word matters
In poetry and prose
But when they fall from your lips
Their importance grows
I don't know if you're aware
But I hang on every word
Every single sentence
And every syllable heard
Your words they make me feel good
They make me feel bold
They make me feel like Superman
When they take ahold
Every time you talk to me
Every word you've said
Is playing on repeat
On the playlist in my head
The most important words
Can be the simplest, I find
The most important one to me
Is when you called me 'mine'

Autumn Waits

The days grow short
And the nights grow long
Autumn is coming
Singing its song
Leaves will turn
And fall to the ground
Time and again
Piled in a mound
Hot apple cider
And hoodies galore
Long evening snuggles
And so much more
Dropping temps
And crisp morning air
My fingers twirling
Through wisps of your hair
Harvest moon's beauty
Lights up the night
Wrapped in my arms
I hold you so tight
There's so much loving
On nights cool and clear
Is it any wonder
It's my favorite time of year

Favorite

Waking next to you
Is my favorite thing in life
It supersedes all struggle
Torment, woe, or strife
But then again our breakfast
Not long after alarm clock's ring
Is utterly fantastic
So that's my favorite thing
Of course there's lunchtime fun
In the middle of the day
There's really nothing better
That's my favorite, I say
What about the evening?
When we cook together and dine
That's absolutely the best
That's the favorite of mine
But tucking you in at night
That's a sacred time for me
Cuddling with you and sleeping
It's my favorite thing, you see
But it seems that I've forgotten
All the moments in between
The looks, the laughs, the back and forth
That's my favorite scene
Apparently I can't decide
Just what's my favorite part
I guess I'll say it's loving you
And giving you my heart

Bleeding Wound

I'll lay here with an open wound
Pouring words instead of blood
No way to stem the flow
Only paper to stop the flood
Heart and soul on display
Vulnerable as a waif
All my faith is placed in you
And I know you'll keep me safe
The world demands an image pure
All things neatly on a shelf
My chaos won't behave that way
But with you I am myself
All my life I hid my wild
Locked away with key and latch
But at last that door's unlocked
In you I found my perfect match

Confide

A place in the sun
Where we can just be
Laying together
My baby and me
Watching clouds pass
Enjoying the day
Fingers entwined
Content where we lay
The best part of us
That can't be denied
It's not really secret
But in you I confide
It doesn't matter
Whatever we do
The one thing I want
Is to do it with you

Reversal

I feel you in the moonlight
Dancing on my skin
Waking my desire
And the animal within
I feel you in my dreamscapes
Waltzing through my mind
Your presence ever welcome
Loving, sweet and kind
I feel you in my beating heart
Pushing fire through my veins
You started an inferno
That sweeps across my plains
I've opened up myself to you
Mind and body and soul
And in return you've done the same
Reversing every role
Your moonlight graces my tides
And they reflect your glow
As you awake my beast inside
Your fangs begin to show
You walk with me hand in hand
Across our fevered dreams
Where my fire warms your soul
As it seeps between our seams
We're connected across dimensions
And places none can see
And nothing is as intimate
As the love between you and me

Magical Might

There's no other magic
Greater than your own
It started as stardust
To a universe it's grown
Your magical impact
Everywhere to see
It colors our world
And salvages me
It makes me feel happy
Makes me a better man
I've absorbed your lessons
Every chance that I can
You don't seem to know
How powerful you are
My witchy woman
My shining star
All of your power
All your star shine
Makes me forever
Glad that you're mine

Shadow And The Sun

I cast a long shadow
For you are my sun
Right next to me
Forever it runs
Your brilliant light
Makes my whole world glow
Burning so bright
Wherever we go
Like a flower I bloom
Under your gaze
My uplifted soul
My colors ablaze
Only your shimmer
Can light up the moon
Caressing my nights
Waning too soon
Ever the wonder
My magical one
Everything's perfect
Under your sun

Quarry

If you were the predator
And I were your prey
It would be really hard
To want to run away
The lure of your beauty
Your scent on the wind
Drawing me closer
The hunt can begin
Your skills as a hunter
Aren't easy to match
My only hope
Is you keep what you catch
You're closing in
And taking me down
Running your quarry
Into the ground
Now that you've got me
What will you do?
I'll ask you one question
Just who captured who?

Influential

If you were a flower
And I were a bee
I'd make you bloom
For the whole world to see
If I were a songbird
You'd be my song
I'd sing at full volume
All the day long
If I were the sunrise
I'd share my sky
With your shining moon
As you pass me by
If you were a river
And I were the sea
You would forever
Be part of me
You're all of these things
And so many more
Your magical pull
Brings me ashore
You and your magic
Influences mine
And it will continue
For the rest of all time

Time Tested

I have but one request to make
Before I pray my soul to take
Before I lay me down to rest
Let me pass this final test
Once upon a lovely night
The hand of Fate produced a light
Our souls were to each other bound
Our life together thus was found
Nevermore we'd be alone
Side by side, throne by throne
A thousand lives Fate did give
A thousand more we've yet to live
My final test is here at last
I have no doubt that I will pass
It doesn't even take much nerve
To forever love you as you deserve

Standing Tall

You have a warrior's heart
And the spirit to which it's paired
There's nothing that you cannot do
No challenge will be spared
There's no supervillain
Whose scheme is worth its weight
That can keep you from your victory
They can't overpower Fate
For me it's such an honor
To battle at your side
To face a foe as equals, love
Animates my pride
There's nothing that I won't endure
No torture yet devised
That will keep me from you evermore
Through a thousand future lives
You were always meant for great things
That I believe is true
And the best thing in this life I've found
Is standing tall with you

Close Comfort

When world gets crazy
And out of control
We need a calming
Place we can go
It's fortunate for us
We need not go far
For you are my moonlight
My twinkling star
Waiting for you
Arms opened wide
Your safe space
Your quiet inside
Your head on my shoulder
Where I place a kiss
We live for moments
As peaceful as this
And part of the magic
Springing from thee
Is that comforting you
Also comforts me

HA Blackwood

Interstellar

Collisions
Like objects in space
We careen off of others
Spinning away
In directions unknown
Gravity
Sometimes holds us
In one place
Until we find the strength
To break free
Intercept
We find the thing
Our heart sought
And suddenly
The journey makes sense

Regardless

No matter what the day or time
I'm always grateful that you're mine
Morning, noon, or depth of night
Within your arms you hold me tight
Winter, summer, spring or fall
I love you completely through them all
All year round my favorite thing
Is the unconditional love you bring
Time of day or season's change
Nothing alters our love's range
A world apart or side by side
This love of ours is one sweet ride

Freedom

I see across a span of time
The lifetimes we have lived
Miles traveled and journeys long
And the love and joy we give
Through the ages we have run
Always us against the rest
Souls together through it all
We've never failed any test
Who knows what the future holds
Or the trials we may face
All I know is you and I
Will take them all with poise and grace
When the universe shall end
Side by side I know we'll be
Facing Fate with heads held high
From a love that set us free

Believer

I believe
There's one true love
Above all others you will find
I believe
Your soul is paired
And to its mate it will bind
I believe
They travel time
In mortal bodies so aligned
I believe
The hand of Fate
Held with love can be so kind
I believe
I've found in you
My true mate forever twined
In you, my love
I believe

HA Blackwood

Yes

Our days and nights
Cuddled and warm
Can be really sweet
Or a passionate storm
The feel of your body
Pressed into mine
Fills up my soul
And warms me like wine
Lazily laying
Together, entwined
A casual reminder
I'm yours and you're mine
Breath upon skin
An exciting caress
Nothing to the thrill
Of a single word - YES

Nightlife

Some people like to drink a lot
And others like to dance til dawn
While some prefer a quiet night
To a dangerous liaison
Running with the hottest crowd
To some is an important fest
While others like the easy life
And leave the running to the rest
It matters not to me one bit
If our nights are in, or out
If we decide to watch a show
Or in a club we twist and shout
The secret to our happy life
It doesn't matter what we do
No matter what our escapades
They're perfect when it's me and you

Multimedia

Lightning flash and thunder roar
Rain crash down on desert shore
Wind will blow and snow can fall
Our love will outlast it all
Water boil and cauldron bubble
Witch's wart and wolfman's stubble
Vampire's tooth and mummy's wrap
Nothing ever sets us back
Criminal minds or CSI
Ancient Aliens in the sky
Supernatural or Dawson's Creek
Your pure heart is all I seek
Reading books or watching shows
Where you lead is where I'll go
For you and I are hand in glove
Heart to heart, stone in love

The Way I Feel

When you're lying next to me
I feel like a king among men
And every time you kiss my lips
It's like I'm being crowned again
When you look into my eyes
I can feel you touch my soul
The universe then expands
As it feels our love grow
When I say your name aloud
It thrills me to my very bones
No music has a sweeter sound
Or makes me feel like I'm home

Monstrous

Dracula is a monster
Most misunderstand
He simply loved a woman
More than God had planned
When she was taken
Unjustly from his side
He cast aside the mortal life
To search for his lost bride
Across a sea of time
He waited to make his move
But a fearful populace
Had to bust his groove
I only bring this up
Because I see his point
If the same thing happened here
I'd tear apart this joint
I'd become a monster
And do what I had to do
To break through the obstacles
And find my way to you

Location, Location, Location

If I lived beneath the sea
I would want you there with me
Swimming with the little fish
Side by side would be my wish
If I lived above the clouds
Singing your praises way out loud
I would be right next you
As we fly through skies of blue
But I live here on earth
A perfect place, for what it's worth
I can travel near or far
And always you're my guiding star

Rarified

No one ever told me
Love could be like this
Is this feeling rare enough
That so few reminisce
The feeling of the thread
Woven through my chest
Connecting me to you
Our true love expressed
Never had I expected
To feel this magic pull
The astral plane connection
That keeps my heart so full
If this Fated bond of ours
Is such an uncommon sight
We cannot waste a moment
And must love with all our might
No wasted opportunities
To mock the gods above
I'll give you every piece of me
And be worthy of this love

Fragments

Every moonbeam holds a piece of you
Each blooming flower's petals do too
Fragments of you decorate my world
I hear your voice singing in the wind
In silence I can hear it again
Nature's song is all about my girl.
I see your eyes in the sky so blue
Your smile like the sun shining through
Each perfect day burned into my soul
Your brilliant mind to me it sings
Of your heart and the love it brings
Your fragments sum make my life whole

Let's Play A Game

You took my breath and ran from me
Knowing I would give chase
You gave it back with a kiss
Hands astride my face
I chased you up to space and back
Knowing you could be caught
I took back my breath with your lips on mine
That touch was all that I sought
Away once more around the world
Our game it would begin
Galaxy bound to worlds unknown
You captured my breath again
I never imagined in my wildest dreams
I'd have a love like this
You lead me around the universe
To catch me with love's true kiss
Back on earth and in my arms
On each other we do depend
Deeply in love and playing this game
We never want to end

Lost and Found

I want to get lost in you
And wander so deep
I never find my way out
I want you to wander so deep
Into me that you get lost
And can't find your out
We'll meet in the middle
Bathed in moonlight and magic
And realize
This is where we belonged
All along

Privateers

The thundering of my heart
Drowns out any storm
The fire in my veins
Will always keep you warm
The fever of your touch
Is the cure for all my ails
The breath of your sweet kiss
Puts the wind into my sails
Our passion merged together
Is like a flag unfurled
Together, my perfect love
We'll conquer the whole world

Well Read

You read me like a book
I'm helpless
As you turn my pages
Hopeful
You enjoy the tale told
Excited
As you pick up the pace
Ecstatic
When you reach for the
Next volume
As you continue the story
And dive into me again

Origins

Some of my poems involve
The sun and moon and stars
While others are on the sea
Or mountaintops or cars
But there's one common thread
That runs my work through
It should come as no surprise
That common thread is you
You're the inspiration
The target of my prose
The one for whom my ink does flow
The color in my rose
From the moment that I wake
Until I fall asleep in bed
Visions of you are dancing
Forever in my head
No matter what the setting
Date or place or time
It's your magic presence
That makes my rhythm rhyme

Protection

I get the feeling you need me
In more than our usual style
When I feel your sense of longing
Hidden by your smile
You need to be protected
And held within my arms
To lower your defenses
Yet never come to harm
And I will say I've got you
And mean it through and through
I'll guard you with my life itself
So none will misconstrue
We always have each other
We always have our backs
We always know the other
Will protect us from attack
So when you're feeling tired
And need to remove your crown
Know that I will be there
When you set it down
When the day is over
And it's only you and me
Lay your head upon my chest
And set your worries free

Idiomatic

Home is where the heart is
Or so the story goes
But when my home is in your heart
I go where you propose
Love is in the air, they say
When couples do abound
But your love burns inside my veins
Once our fate was found
It takes two to tango
Is a popular refrain
It takes two do lots of things
And do them all again
You won't steal my thunder
Or put my back against the wall
Some go the extra mile
For you I'll go them all
We're two peas in a pod
You're my cup of tea
To put it in a nutshell
You're everything to me

Safe Harbor

Give me your storms
Raging and fierce
I'll take them all and more
Steer toward my light
Steady and bright
Crash your ship on my shore
No matter the tempest
That splinters the night
With winds that wail and moan
You'll have safe harbor
Forever my love
And a place to always call home

Influenced

You have an influence over me
My body and my brain
It's not that you control my moves
Perhaps I should explain
I'm not a marionette
Where you get to pull my strings
Though I'd like being tied to you
Among many other things
I'm not some sort of muppet
Where your hand can work my mouth
But I do enjoy my mouth on you
And all things north and south
The influence that you have
Isn't difficult to see
It's the way you raise my heart rate
When you look at me
It's the way you're on my mind
Whenever we're apart
Or how you set my world aglow
When you let me in your heart
I told you at the top
You influence body and brain
And if we lived this life a thousand times
I wouldn't change a thing

Heartbeats

Your heart belongs to me
Is not an idle claim
And in point of fact
You could say the same
You gave to me your heart
When you fell for me
Reluctantly at first
Then so gleefully
And the moment that I knew
I was in love with you
I promptly gave you mine
There was nothing else to do
There are people who think
It's just a turn of phrase
They've clearly never felt
A lover's tender gaze
They've never felt the ache
When two lovers part
It resides inside the chest
And can only be the heart
As for you and me
And the hearts that we did trade
I've never had a doubt
It's the best bargain ever made
We're both our heart's true match
We'll search for love no more
I'll eternally guard your precious heart
And mine is yours forevermore

Elixir

You ignite my fires and let them burn
Warming your soul at my side
Your own flame burns brighter and lights up my world
And oh what a wonderful ride
You inspire such magic to pour out of me
Just by being yourself
Your beautiful presence a witch's elixir
And such fun behaviors compelled
My life's ever better since you've been involved
I know this without any doubt
You lift up my soul and my heart beats for you
Your name to the heavens I shout
If ever a love was Fated to be
It surely is yours and mine
All that we are just lines up so true
And will for the remainder of time

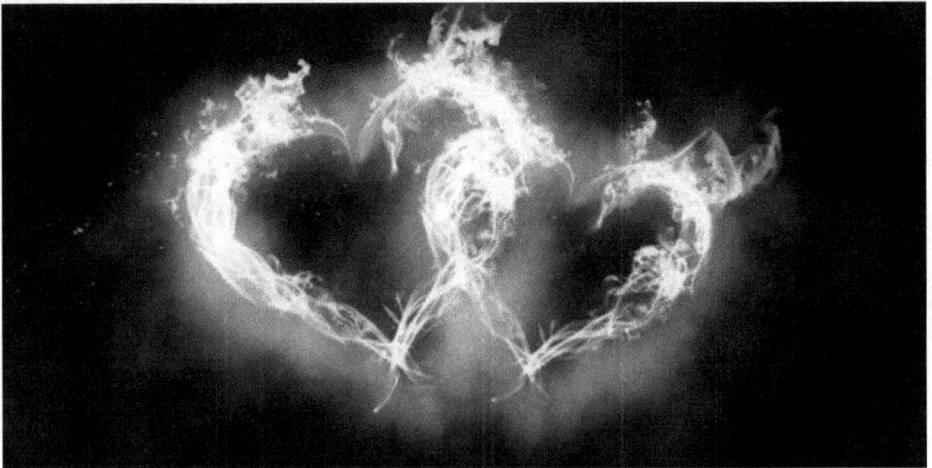

Coveted Coven

Witches have gotten a bad rap it seems
Through the ages described as evil and mean
Eating children, casting spells
Dressed all in black and colored green
The men who accused them throughout history
Were as mean and evil as the witches they'd see
Lying, conniving, and sadistic too
Duplicitous men, as bad as can be
All extra power wielded by man
Is as good or evil as the intent of their hand
Witch or warlock, it matters not
Only the ultimate goal of their plan
Witchy women are just fine by me
No need for trials, just let them be
If they're naughty by nature
Karma will get them, just wait and see
So boil, boil toil and trouble
Fire burn and cauldron bubble
Foxy witch get on your broom
And fly over here on the double

Cardinal Prayer

I look to the east and I see you there
Where the sun claims the sky from the moon
And a new day is born from the night
I look to the north and I see you there
Where snow quiets the land and the auroras
Color the sky like the rules of nature don't apply
I look to the south and I see you there
Unclaimed lands abound
Mystery and adventure await
I look to the west and I see you there
The horizon devouring the sun
Giving the moon back her birthright
It matters not which direction I look
I find evidence of you
Your beauty, your magic, our love
Unbound, wild, and free

Twinkling

I wonder where the time goes
When I'm lost in you
It speeds by so much faster
Than anything else I do
I wonder if the stars align
What will happen then
Will all our dreams fall into place
As if they've always been?
I wonder what the day will bring
I wonder at the night
I wonder at the starry sky
Twinkling so bright
I wonder about so many things
Questions great and small
But one thing that I know for sure
You're the most wondrous thing of all

Death Dealing

Death comes calling
When your debt is due
There's no striking a deal
Or pulling off a coup
He harvests your soul
When he swings his blade
Your time's up no matter
How hard you've prayed
You see his shadow
And think you can run
But he's swifter than you
And the chase is his fun
I plan to face him
With you at my side
When he sees our magic
He'll let that debt slide
He'll check his ledger
And see that we've paid
An advance on that debt
And we're unafraid
I don't say this to mock him
Or make light of his work
I'm not trying to cheat
Or make him look like a jerk
But in this spooky season
Thin is death's veil
He knows our story
And Fate's role in our tale
He'll stand aside
For a love like ours
Played out on earth
But forged in the stars

Newton's Law

The earth holds the moon
Safe in its grasp
Keeping her from hurtling through space
She pulls the tides
That give this rock life
Neither exists without the other's grace
So it is with us
You're safe in my arms
Yet it's your pull that moves my tide
One doesn't exist
But for the grace of the other
Perfectly balanced and giving us life
My lightning and storms
And your stardust and light
Building our love and lighting our fire
Two souls as one
On this journey together
Lighting our way with blinding desire

All That Remains

What remains when
Time has had her way
And washed away youth
Bones brittle
Muscles sagged
Skin wrinkled
Strength flagged
What remains then?
You and I remain
Never diminished
In the eyes of the other
Never lessened
In each other's arms
What remains
At the end of the day?
We do.
And we always will.

Time Travel

There was a time
Where I couldn't see
The kind of joy
You've brought to me
There was a time
That I never knew
Fate had her plans
To bring me to you
For the rest of our time
Now that we know
We have forever
To let our love grow
Time keeps on ticking
Like it's apt to do
For us it's no matter
As our wish has come true

HA Blackwood

Living the Dream

Awake or asleep
A dilemma it seems
Either way
You're here with me
But which would I rather
If I had my choice
Live in a dream
Or hear your voice
Soar through the air
Fingers entwined
Or feel the thrill
When you say you're mine
It's not a contest
As much as it seems
For life with you, baby
Is living my dreams

Teamwork

Everywhere I go
Everything I do
Always has a connection
That brings me back to you
Doing the dishes
Or walking the dog
Folding laundry
Or the workday's slog
Shopping for groceries
One of my favorite things
With you in the aisles
One of my favorite things
A lot of life's tasks
May seem mundane
But being with you
They're just not the same
I love every chore
That I get to do
Because I am blessed
To do them with you

Meteorology

Sunshine in the morning
Is how I start my day
Always when I see your face
Even if skies are gray
I can wear a hat and coat
In case the chill sinks in
But your heart it keeps me warm
I'll never be cold again
Rain or snow or sleet or hail
Blowing winds and lightning too
Any storm is perfect now
If I can weather it with you
So huddle in and hunker down
And let the shrill winds blow
We're immune to nature's whims
When we're snugged from tip to toe

Magick

Magic is not
Just for card tricks and shows
It's not just illusionists
Wearing sequins and bows
Those are mere parlor tricks
Compared to our brand
To our mystic connection
As we walk hand in hand
It's the way that you know me
As I know myself
How you know what to say
To make my heart melt
Or how I know
Just what you need
Time after time
It's magick indeed
But it's mostly the way
Fate worked her plan
That you, perfect woman
Would be paired with this man

Siren

Lyrics make the song
Music brings it to life
The vocalist gives it a soul
My life has always had lyrics
And music only I could hear
But you
Oh, you
You heard the music
And you sang the song
As if you knew
It was written for you
All along

Sheep's Clothing

The supernatural wolf
Has a complex role in our lives
The werewolf and the shifter
Are on opposite sides
Man at most times
The werewolf is a beast
No control over his nature
You are his feast
The shifter is different
He changes at will
And maintains his mind
And sexiness still
One leaves your body
Bloody with gore
Ravished by the other
You're begging for more
Just know what you've got
When facing your foes
Don't forfeit your life
When you forego your clothes

Just You

I say you're amazing
You say you're just you
And you're right.
Just you sets my world on fire
Igniting the blood in my veins
The forge of my soul
Kindling the fire of my
Unconditional love
And passion for you
Just you brightens the darkest night
Shining your moonlight
Casting away the shadows
Making my heart feel safe
Before you curl up inside
Just you spreads your magic
Across the land
Blooming flowers
Brighter sunrises
And making me strive
To be the man
Who deserves
Just you

All The Small Things

It's always the little things
That mean so much to me
A look, a touch, a whispered word
Fit like a lock and key
These interstitial moments
Are intimate to their core
They bind us tight together
And help weather any storm
Every point of contact
Feels good and true
Strengthening the bond
That exists between me and you
I'll never miss a moment
Whether large or small
To build on our connection
I'll forever give my all
In times of stress and worry
These little things abound
They help to soothe our fragile nerves
When the other's not around
Flowers, notes and letters
An I love you here and there
There's no incorrect way
To show how much we care
When the day is over
We'll be oh so glad
To know we gave each other
Everything we had

Intangibles

Sometimes the best connections
Come from things you cannot touch
A smoldering look across the room
Can never be too much
Or when I hear your voice
When you're far away
And how it makes my heart beat
Always makes my day
I love you's at midnight
Updates from the road
Every single contact
Lightens a heavy load
No matter the intangible
That comes into my view
I love every reminder
That I belong to you

Contact

My gloriously beautiful woman
Where do I begin
Those eyes that look so happy
That smile that does me in
Poetry in motion
With every image sent
Every breath is stolen
My soul to you is sent
You can't know the effect
You have upon the world
But through eyes that see you clear
We're the grains inside your pearl
Every single contact
You have through your day
You spread a little magic
Making the world a better place
My heart it beats just for you
And it always will
With you I'll spend my entire life
I'll never get my fill

Anywhere

Some moments you want to last forever
And of course they never do
Like waking in the dead of night
And being softly kissed by you
Silky lips grazing mine
Sweet breath upon my face
A hand upon either cheek
I lose track of time and place
I try to move but you hold me still
And kiss me slowly with soft intent
A magic moment filled with grace
I open my eyes to your lingering scent
A dream, I find, to my dismay
Your delicious lips on mine
I wish I never had to wake
But alas that is life's design
It makes those moments worth so much more
A fading dream, an answered prayer
A waking thought solidifies
Woman, I'll follow you anywhere

Beyond Time And Space

What does forever mean
In the context of you and I
Is it time or distance
Like the limitless blue sky?
I can see forever
When I look into your eyes
Sapphire blue for eternity
Far beyond earths skies
Or is it a temporal measure
Like from the dawn of time
For that's at least how long
Your heart has been all mine
I know forever is more
Than until the day I die
For our love is immortal
Over eons we shall glide
Forever is a feeling
Forever is a place
Forever is holding you in my arms
With that smile on your face
It's knowing you belong to me
And that the reverse is true
Forever is each place and time
I get to be with you

Connected

All that I am
All that I know
Is connected to you
And bathed in your glow
Your voice on the wind
My heart in the sky
Your lips on my neck
And your hand on my thigh
Pulling you close
Our bodies so warm
My thundering pulse
Our gathering storm
Pressure is building
Lightning flashes
Our bodies writhing
Our wave crashes
Over and over
We're tossed on the shore
Helpless to fight it
But begging for more
All that I know
All that I am
Is connected to you
For that is Fate's plan

Trouble Brewing

In a frenzy the miles fell
As I was running out of time
Closer to you at the tolling bell
I had to make you mine
Cursed by witch's ire
Doomed to fall far short
I'll be tried and convicted
In this witch's coven court
She set for me a task
Impossible it seemed
To go and find true love
As she exists inside my dreams
As the clock struck midnight
Fewer peals remain
When over the horizon
You came into frame
I ran as fast as I could
And you did so as well
Ever closing the distance
Against the pealing bell
You threw yourself headlong
The circumstance so grave
You wrapped your arms around me
My life and soul you saved
With just a single kiss
You proved that you were mine
And saved me from that witches curse
In just the nick of time
Always will you save me, love
From trouble, should it brew
For what that witch forgot to check
Was that I belong to you

Traveling

Time has no meaning
When you're lost inside a dream
Minutes can cover hours
Or days and weeks it seems
It's just the same with distance
Like bending time and space
I can take us anywhere
To feel your hands upon my face
Though I am not an astronaut
Master of space and time
I can bring us together here
In the space that is my mind
There's no limit to where we go
Or what we want to do
The only thing that I require
Is that it's done with you
A puff of smoke
A wisp of steam
And suddenly we're gone my love
Traveling on a dream

Relocation

Of all the places I could go
Around this lovely world
Mountain high or valley low
I could give any place a whirl
I could try the desert's heat
Or the arctic's bitter freeze
A temperate clime with sweeping views
That bring me to my knees
Spin the globe and pick a spot
And that is where I'll go
It matters not if I speak the tongue
Or the language I do not know
Leave the world an address to find
Or from them all I'll hide
The perfect place on this blue globe
Is where I'm at your side

Homecoming

Walking through the streets of my mind
Looking for a place to fit in
Everything's cold and the streets were grey
My grip on reality was wearing thin
I followed a path I'd never seen
Drawn by a force unknown
Farther away than I've ever been
Yet feeling close to home
I passed by a door and glanced inside
Taken aback by the view
I pulled it open to see what's there
And was flooded by the colors of you
Warmth and sunshine spilled on out
Changing the world bit by bit
I never knew there was a perfect soul
But I had just discovered it
You smiled at me and touched my face
And wondered what took so long
You didn't know it was me who'd come
Until you heard my heart's song
The one that only you could hear
The one only you could understand
It would mean this heart was yours
You only had to take my hand
You reached out your hand to mine
As you touched me, I let out a gasp
I could see you clearly now
And knew that I was home at last

Monster mash

All Hallow's Eve
Death's thinnest veil
All monsters come out
Ready to to wail
We'll run together
Dodging their chase
I'll be your decoy
You be my ace
I'll choke the wolfman
With your silver chain
While you catch the Creature
And flush him down the drain
As Frankenstein lurches
And makes the ground quake
I'll sneak up on Dracula
I'll serve him a stake
You get jumper cables
On old Frank's bolts
And I'll zap him good
With 90,000 volts
The mummy is easy
For you and me
We just unravel his wrap
When we turn to flee
The monsters don't phase us
As we run and hide
For they don't know
About our monsters inside

There Is You

At the end of the day
When work's gone away
My brain is spent
And I need to vent
There is you
When I wake in the night
From dreams filled with fright
And I can't close my eyes
Fearing nightmare's reprise
There is you
When I wake in the morn
From sleep I am torn
I get to choose
Get up or snooze
There is you
There is an answer
When life turns drear
When energy ebbs
There's nothing to fear
For there's you

Eternal Flame

I always wonder
Where does the time go
Days and weeks flyby
Relentless, never slows
All time is relative
As Einstein declared
Since I've met you
In your vortex I'm snared
In the outside world
Time slows to a crawl
But in here with you
It's balls to the wall
Every second together
Is precious as hell
I wish they went slower
So we could savor them well
I will take comfort
In this simple truth
Our love is eternal
And I get to spend it with you

What I need

There are things in life
That all men need
Things we can touch
And things we can see
Food and shelter
Are high on the list
Maslow's ranking
Can give you the gist
But other things
Can't be held
Or quantified
As though they're geld
A touch, a look
A word or phrase
Your unique beauty
Which goes on for days
A soul connection
For which I'd bleed
Is tops among
The things I need
A heart to love
A reason to be
A love like yours
To set me free

No Limit

I'd wade through fields
Of fire and blood
To stand next to you
One more time
I'd suffer the circles of hell
And all their torment
To hear your voice
Sing in my ear
I'd swim across oceans
Of sirens and monsters
Just to see the sun
Shine on your face
I'd scale mountains
Cross rivers
Forage deep into
Jungles unknown
If it meant always
Being able to say
You are mine

Everywhere We Go

Everywhere I go
You come with me
In my thoughts
In my heart
Everywhere I go
There you are
Everywhere you go
I go with you
Your mind
Your soul
Bring me along
Everywhere you go
There I am
There's no distance
We cannot bridge
When two souls connect
Everywhere we go
There we are

Playing Favorites

Of all the ways to be intimate
Physically, bodies writhing
Moaning, losing control
Mentally, knowing each other
In tune with wants and needs
Casually, touching and teasing
Effortlessly spending time
Intellectually, challenging
Each other to think and grow
Emotionally, sharing feelings
Connected at their core
Of all the ways to be intimate
My favorite one
Is all of them

Light Show

There's a light in your eyes
That rivals the sun
A fire inside
That can't be outrun
The light from your soul
Through the surface it shines
Irrepressible beauty
Unlimited rhymes
Like the sun in the sky
You glow from within
Lighting the world
To show where you've been
Your inner light
Shines for all to see
And each day it makes you
More beautiful to me

Days Gone Bye

All the long days gone by
With plans unmet
Time squandered
And full of regret
Don't mean a thing
In the glow of your light
Since Fate intervened
The future is so bright
Now each day
Is packed full of you
All the time in the world
To do what we do
We fill all our time
With truckloads of fun
Everything we can think of
Under the sun
Days long gone by
Have so much value
For each one of them
Helped lead me to you

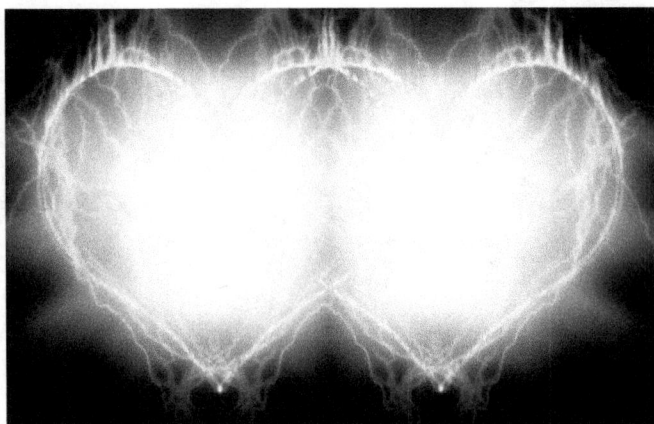

Ageless

Sunny days
And moonlit nights
Melodies
Of ancient rites
Magick cast
And spells abound
Across the ages
Our love is sound
Burning fire
Bubbling pot
Hidden ways
That time forgot
Over the eons
Our souls are bound
The ways of old
In us are found
On astral planes
That none can see
Live you and I
Eternally

Valuables

Of all the things I've longed to have
Or who I've longed to be
The most important thing is love
And the best person to be is me
You've shown me what true love is like
You're shown me a better way
The value of authenticity
And not caring what others say
The value of our self is weighed
In our own eyes and mind
You've taught me to be a better man
And to myself be kind
Of all the things I've longed to have
Or who I've longed to be
The thing worth having is you to love
For you have set me free

To Every Season

Clear blue skies
And sunny days
Misty mornings
Filled with haze
Springtime nights
So crystal clear
Snowy eves
With autumn's cheer
No matter what
It does outside
I know that you'll be
At my side
Summer splendor
Or winter's view
'Tis always the season
To be with you

Overnight

Evening times
Sweet reprise
Luscious lips
Soulful eyes
Cuddled close
Two as one
Resting now
'Til morning's sun
Sound asleep
Happy pair
Dreams abound
In cold night air
Alarm's ring
Time to rise
First morning's kiss
Our greatest prize

Everlasting

A tiger can't change its stripes
Nor a leopard its spots
They're stuck with their colors
Whether they like it or not
Other things occur
In an autonomic fashion
Like the beating of my heart
And the fury of my passion
The moment that our magnets clicked
To our conscious minds unknown
The hand of Fate reached down
And a seed was sown
Like breathing in and out
Which happens on its own
Our binding love for each other
Over time has grown
Tiger stripes and leopard spots
Breaths and heartbeats galore
Add to this list of certain things
Our love lasting evermore

Trustworthy

It matters not what threats may come
Or what our enemies may do
I have no concern for them
For I place my trust in you
They can throw me to the wolves
Or leave me for dead
I have faith in you my love
That you'll save my life instead
You can lead my armies
And rule at my side
Take delight as our enemies
All run and hide
From the moment we met
I instantly knew
No matter the problem
I could rely on you

Language Lessons

Venustas, indurata et cerebra
Beauty, brawn and brains
In English or in Latin
You have them just the same
Gentilezza, passione e amore
Kindness, passion and love
These aren't things you purchase
You're gifted from above
Corps, âme et coeur
Body, soul and heart
Things that can't be taken
I gave you from the start
In a world full of languages
Different, yet the same
Pones mi corazón en llamas
You set my heart aflame
The hand of Fate has blessed us
Given us lifetimes to explore
It matters not the language used
Our love is forevermore

Moonlight

Under the moon
Bathed in your glow
You will find me
Waiting for you
Shifter, shifted
Ready to run
Ready to hunt
Waiting for you
Across the moor
A plaintive wail
Turns to a howl
Calling to me
Hackles rise
Haunches tense
Paws in motion
Coming for you
Top of the rise
Glowing eyes
Tooth and tail
We are home

Primal

Dark desires hidden away
For fear of revealing too much
Too soon
About what lies beneath
Monsters locked inside
To hide what people think
Is weird
And unacceptable
But desires drive us
Give us reasons
To move forward
And thrive
Monsters are really just us
In our raw and primal forms
You taught me to be myself
That we're all beautiful
And in the process
You set me free

Wolfpack

Once again around the sun
Another year is almost done
With you, my love, I've had such fun
Praise to Fate that you're the one
Around the world and circle back
The two of us our beasts will track
Showing strength where the other lacks
Is why we make a perfect pack
Battles fought had been our own
Through bloodied scar and broken bone
From a seed our love has grown
Nevermore to be alone

Compass

Never before and never again
Will there be a love so true
In this life and all to come
My compass only points to you
Our souls were paired from the dawn of time
Ten thousand lives won't be enough
Such a fire in us has been alit
A hurricane could never snuff
Greater still our love it grows
The universe cannot contain
Expand it must to make more room
So this love of ours can reign
When tale's told and time does end
We'll be there, hand in hand
United then as ever before
Together forever, as Fate had planned

Thanksgiving

There's not a day that passes
That I don't talk to Fate
And give her my undying thanks
For making you my mate
For taking her red thread
And giving us each an end
Ensuring you'd be my lover
My confidant and friend
We each have walked a path
That led us here and now
She knew we'd find each other
We just don't understand how
Now that we're together
A moment won't go to waste
We're going to enjoy each other
No matter the time or place
The world is ours to conquer
If only we want to dare
With your hand in mine, my love
It doesn't stand a prayer

Night Music

A moan like a bassoon
Echoes o'er the moors
A bellow and a warning
Better get indoors
Thundering footsteps
Tympani uncontrolled
Danger getting closer
Blood turns ice cold
Just as bony fingers
Set upon my spine
I wake up from this nightmare
Your body pressed to mine
You tell me that you've got me
It will always be okay
You'll take the frights my mind creates
And scare them all away
It's hard to take a nightmare
And digest just what it means
But I'll fear them never more
For you're the woman of my dreams

Making Time

Clouded eyes tell a story
And rain cascades down a cheek
Time has taken youth's glory
And still your presence makes me weak
I won't lament an empty page
Unwritten stories of things we'd do
Not a moment was wasted there
Each one a treasure spent with you
Time is a thief that robs us all
Leaving shadows in her wake
A blink of eyes and years go by
Rolling on without a break
But for you and I there's no lost time
Every minute a dream fulfilled
Nothing ever left behind
A thousand years on which to build
A glimpse into the future
With lessons from the past
We have lifetimes yet to live
A fated love that's built to last

Desired

Alone in a crowd
Lost in my mind
The sweet stab of desire
Life's greatest find
Desire for meaning
In love and in life
Desire for freedom
From pain and from strife
Desire for better
Than we have today
Desire for passion
To find us, and stay
Fortunately for us
We know just what we need
And we found in each other
Our desires freed

Relentless

Relentless
The way I'm compelled
To want you
Next to me
To need you
In my arms
Never ending
My desire to
See your smile
Hear your voice
Everlasting
My love
And support
For all things you
Is relentless

Combustible

Love that smolders
And hearts that burn
Passions building
That have no terms
No preconditions
Or wind-borne whims
Just fated souls
Which are all-in
Like two chemicals
That chain react
They combust
Yet emerge intact
Stronger together
Than they could be alone
These fiery souls
Have found their home

Master Plan

I've lived a lot of years
And walked a lot of miles
Endured a lot of hard times
And faced a lot of trials
I've made a lot of choices
Some bad and some oh so good
I always knew at the end of the line
I'd have done the best I could
At the other end of the thread
You had walked your path
You didn't have an easy life
But you kicked a lot of ass
Every challenge faced
Was another lesson learned
Another chance to pass a test
And try not to get burned
Neither of us wondered
What it was all about
We kept one foot in front of the other
And never thought to pout
Little did we realize
There was a master plan
To match the two of us together
My woman and her man
Once the magnets clicked
And we felt the thread pull tight
We knew our choices had been well made
And everything's alright

Force of Attraction

The gravity between us was inevitable
As it's always been
Two hearts drawn together
Time and time again
Before time was time
And the cosmos dark and cold
We have been together
From the creation of our souls
Of all our different forms
I like these the best
I love the way my heart beats
With your head upon my chest
I love the way my fingers feel
When they're laced with yours
The way I'm always drawn to you
Like the sea upon the shore
I love that when I pledge my love to you
You smile every time
And I love how the air vibrates
When you tell me you are mine

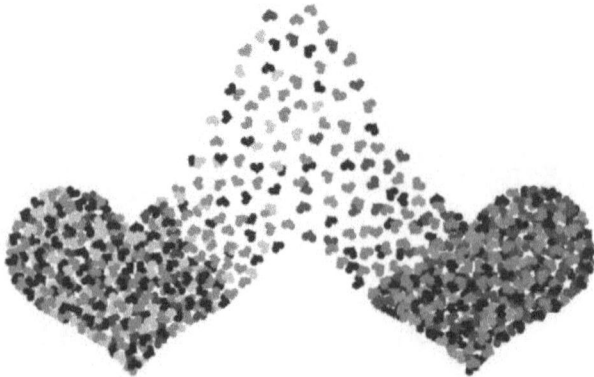

This Thing Called Love

Some say love hurts
And others might agree
But they would have a different
Opinion than me
Love cascades all around you
Bathing you like rain
It soothes you with its touch
And takes away your pain
Love sits up with you
In the night
It holds your hand
And lends you its might
Love is pure
Its intent is true
But if you abuse it
It can turn on you
But I'm a hopeful romantic
Helped by fate above
She led me to my fated mate
So I believe in a thing called love

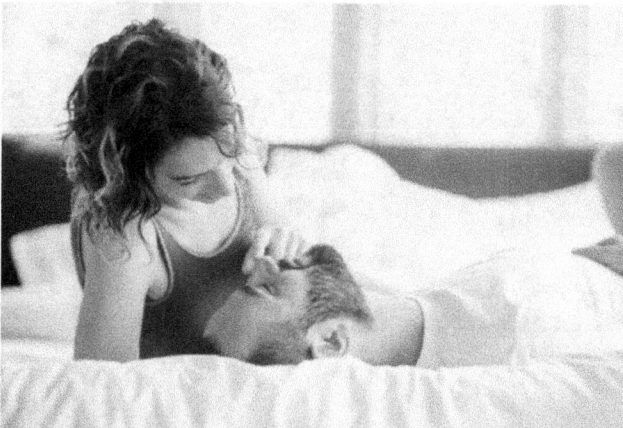

Story Written

Sunlight never shines as bright
As your smile in the darkest night
Glorious songbirds when they rejoice
Don't sound as sweet as your voice
Wormholes fold both space and time
But I'll spend forever at your side
Around you moods and spirits lift
Your open heart is your greatest gift
When it's all been done and said
Our story written and pages read
When I have done all I can do
I hope that I was worthy of you

There Is You

When the clouds sink low
And the cold winds blow
There is you
When the rains settle in
And I'm soaked to the skin
There is you
You keep me warm
In the midst of the storm
You keep me dry
As the squall passes by
When the night takes command
You take my hand
At the end of each day
I look at you and say
There is you

Dreaming

I dream of your silky skin
Brushing against mine
Of loving you in rhythm
And touching you with rhymes
I dream of falling into bliss
And loving you just right
I dream of my body wrapped in yours
Each and every night
I dream of your galactic eyes
Locking on to me
When you hold me in your gaze
You're all that I can see
I dream of your soft fingertips
Dancing across my frame
Since we've come together, love
Nothing's been the same

Hunter Hunted

There's a wolf inside me
Sniffing the wind
Catching your scent
My hunt can begin
I am the hunter
You are my prey
I must be careful
And not give it away
Tracing your steps
I'm drawing near
But I smell excitement
Rather than fear
You've set a trap
It's now plain to see
The wolf inside you
Has been hunting me

Warriors

A dark moon still pulls the tide
And brings the waves to the shore
When we're apart you're still my guide
Bringing me home evermore
Thunderclouds bring the rain
From which most people hide
For us however it keeps us sane
And to the other we each confide
We're no strangers to the night
Or a raging summer storm
It takes more than that to give us a fright
And make us wish we'd not been born
Hand in hand we move ahead
Partners now in love and war
Enemies will wish they're dead
When the two of us kick in their door

Across The Sky

In the dark of night we call to each other
Voices carry across the astral plane
Wings spread, we take to the air
While our bodies on earth remain
Soaring, looping on a thermal wind
Miles pass in the blink of an eye
Reaching speeds we've never known
We race toward each other across the sky
Long ago in ages past
Angels had dominion here
Now it's just for us to own
As we speed across the sky so clear
We sense each other getting close
Even in the darkest night
Our souls compelled to be as one
Powered by our love's pure might
We come together and stars explode
Brand new galaxies giving birth
With you life is heavenly
In these skies as it is on earth

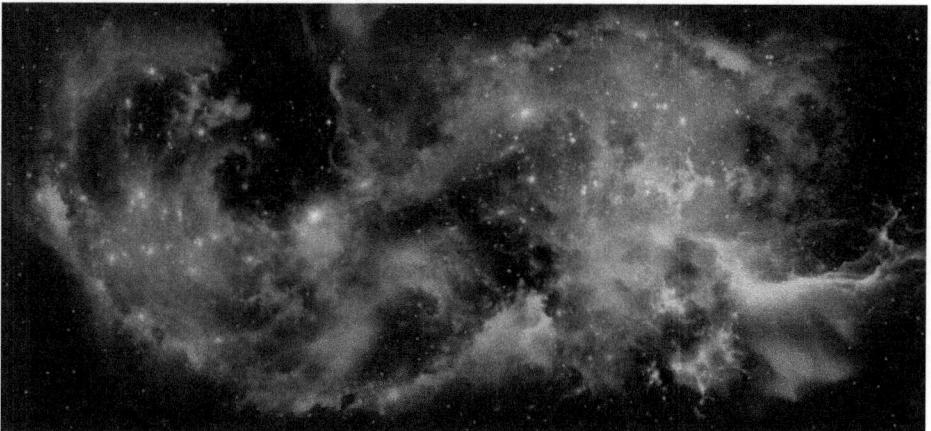

Mastermind

My voice rings out unbidden
In the hollows of your mind
Your body helpless in reaction
Your desires respond in kind
You love the excitement
Of leaving reason behind
Letting loose your baser self
And enjoying what you find
Your voice rings out unbidden
In the hollows of my mind
You lead me into temptation
For I am so inclined
The way our bodies move
Writhe and slip and grind
Moving in synchronicity
Perfectly entwined
It's amazing how we fit
So masterfully aligned
It can only be accounted for
By Fate's perfect design
Never has a fated match
Been so perfectly defined
We'll set the world on fire, love
With our energies combined

Unknown

I never knew that I was lost
Until the day that I was found
I didn't know how deaf I'd been
Until I heard your soul's sweet sound
Once upon a time I thought
I knew all I needed to know
I've since learned that I
Have miles left to grow
Somehow I'd stayed in the dark
About so many things
Including the workings of my heart
And the way it sings
When the stars aligned
And the curtain fell
I knew where I belonged
And who with as well
You've done so much for me
Caused a seismic shift
I hope that when that bell tolls
I've given you that gift

Burning Light

Every place your lips touch me
They leave traces of moonlight
Casting shadows on my body
Illuminating the night
My fire leaves a trail
Where my fingers graze your skin
Heating up your desire
Over and over again
Lost within our passions
Drowning in our need
Bodies tumbling through outer space
Inhibitions freed
Only when we're sated
And our senses have returned
Do we realize how bright your light
Or how delicious was the burn

Yule Be Mine

Reindeer and sleighs
Presents and trees
Passionate lovers
Down on their knees
Bright lights and baubles
Tinsel in strands
Bodies in motion
Wandering hands
Flickering fire
Hearth side delight
Unwrapping our presents
All through the night
No matter the season
Or time of year
We don't need a reason
To hold ourselves near
And this special evening
As we celebrate Yule
The best gift of all
Is a lifetime with you

Painkiller

You're my favorite medicine
The cure for my ills
The sound of your voice
Works better than pills
When my mind works against me
You are the balm
That smooths things over
And keeps me calm
There's no painkiller
Or narcotic drug
That makes me feel better
Than one of your hugs
Regardless what problem
I'm suffering through
It all goes away
With a few words from you

Livin' On A Prayer

I've prayed for a lot of things
Through this life of mine
I've prayed to stop suffering
And for a little more time
I've prayed to end an illness
But also for my personal gain
In the middle of a terrible drought
I've prayed to get some rain
Prayers aren't always answered
Or not in the ways we hope
But the energy is not wasted
I believe it finds its home
You have been the answer
To a prayer I didn't know I'd need
A life changing inspiration
My mind and soul were freed
Now I have just one more prayer
For those who are keeping score
I pray that when the day is done
That I helped answer yours

Amongst The Wild

A bird on the wing
A deer on the hoof
We're called to adventure
The sky is our roof
Out in the woods
Amongst the wild
Human and beast
Now reconciled
Scent on the wind
Paws tear the earth
Hunting in tandem
Shows our true worth
Stronger together
Than we are apart
Two souls entwined
Round our beating hearts
Human and beast
Inside you and me
Together forever
Wild and free

Unburdened

Beneath an infinite sky
Under the moon and stars
I strip you bare of all your burdens
So you can show me who you are
In return I'll show you who I am
Removing any doubt that this is real
I'll strip bare of all my burdens
And my deepest secrets I'll reveal
Beneath an infinite sky
That forms a blanket across the land
We stack our burdens in piles
Outside a home we never knew we had
With the moon and stars as witness
Watching us in the deepest dark
We set ablaze our heap of burdens
And make our home within our hearts

Battlefield

With my head held high
'Neath a devil's sky
I'll battle for you day and night
Piling the dead
As high as my head
Until I'm no longer able to fight
With my sword in my hand
I'll make my last stand
Your name the last word from my lips
With a blade in my side
I'm not afraid to die
I know it's not a one-way trip
I'll give up my soul
For the ferryman's toll
To bring me back to the light
With my head held high
'Neath a devil's sky
I'll love you with all my might

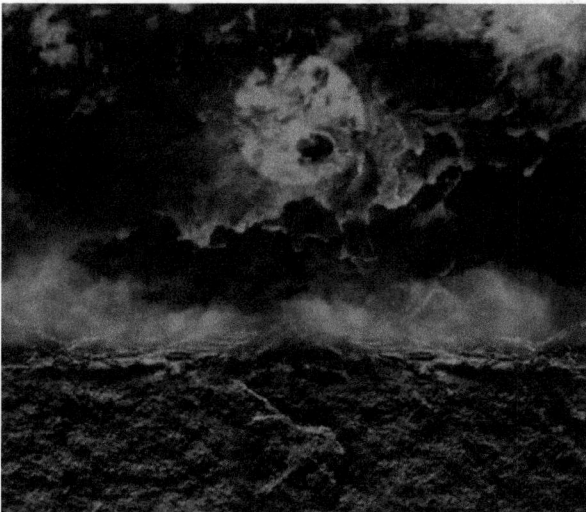

Natural Selection

There was before
And then there's now
All from before you
Is gone somehow
My memory is selective
About what it shows
It brings me the bits
That help write this prose
I have a theory
That the parts that remain
Are those with most meaning
To my heart and my brain
It makes the most sense
If you think it through
The important memories
All involve you

Galactic

Once I knew the stars so well
I'd play with them a little game
Calling each one by their name
Then one perfect, fated night
You fell into my simple life
And nothing's ever been the same
You once loved the moon
With devotion and purity
Still somehow you heard Fate's plea
You fell from the sky with grace and skill
Into my arms as if by will
A shore upon a distant sea
Moon and stars together now
And always will it be this way
Our fears and foes will fly away
Eternal love is what we've found
Born in the stars and lived on the ground
For earths remaining nights and days

Waste Not

I could do without
The aches and pains
That come along with
Advancing age
And the folly of youth
Or the knowledge that
So many opportunities
Were thrown away
Youth is wasted
On the young
An axiom
If not cliché
But there's no alternative
To experience the gain
Of lessons learned
Along the way
It took these years
And lessons galore
To bring us to
The time and place
Where we would meet
And advantage take
So no more moments
Would go to waste

Mystical

Faeries in the night
Wisps that wander
And give us their light
Things of both nightmares and dreams
Showing us the world
Is not as it seems
Portals exist
Hidden doorways
Shrouded in mist
Passages through time
Forward and past
Rhythm and rhyme
Magick is real
Long we have known
Since our love's reveal
Old things and new
I believe in them all
For they led me to you

TBR

I am a book
Whose cover is worn
Binding is cracked
Pages are torn
Spellbinding tales
Of every sort
Adventure and romance
And action galore
I flip through the pages
And read you the best
Hoping with time
You'll read the rest
I'm no bestseller
For the book isn't through
These empty pages
Are waiting for you

Leap Of Fate

Black moonlight shines
As bright
When your soul provides
It's glow
Standing at the edge
Of a cliff
We jump, unafraid
Leap of faith
Leap of Fate
We catch hold
Falling in love
Yours
Mine
Soaring
Eternal
Under the light of your moon

Rescue Me

Life can get crazy
With its frenetic pace
It's something every day
With never a break
Unending to-do lists
And the grind of work
Unrelenting pressure
Can drive you berserk
There is one cure-all
For this rat race
It's nothing real fancy
Wrapped in satin or lace
I just need a moment
To study your face
And the sweet tender rescue
Of your loving embrace

Instinctual

In the dark of night
You're my alpha thought
And its your name that
Spills from my lips
Answering your call
Instinct driving action
I seek your embrace
And the refuge within
Time and again
Forever and beyond
My home will always be
Where your voice calls to me

Shadows

Eyes aglow
Wary, and keen
All tooth and claw
In shadow unseen
Protector mine
Watcher, aware
Waiting, patient
Devil ensnared
Rumbling growl
And hackles arise
Demons attack
To their demise
Run through the dark
Monsters beware
Your disadvantage
You're fighting a pair
Make no mistake
We know what you saw
But she's not alone
With tooth and claw

Sanctuary

There's sanctuary in the knowledge
That in this world, oft dark and malign
A soul like yours not only exists
But is Fate bound to mine

No Guarantees

There are no guarantees
In the span of a life
One can work really hard
And always do right
Yet still get the short straw
When it comes a head
Knocked to the ground
And wishing you're dead
All you can hope for at the end of the day
When you feel as though you've been run through
If you've lived well and the fates are kind
Is to find oneself with a love such as you

Tumblers

Your secrets are hidden
In places unseen
Clues all around
Just meant for me
A kiss is a key
A trust that is earned
Placed in the right spot
So tumblers will turn
Locks fall away
Entrance is gained
One step inside
Nothing is the same
Your secrets are spilled
But I have some too
And I have left clues
Meant only for you

Devil May Care

You and me and the devil make three
But with a smile so pure and a voice so sweet
You're the only devil that I'll ever need
There's an angel on my shoulder watching over me
We'll have to sneak away so she doesn't see
That it's you who brings out the devil in me
The devil made me do it is an oft-used excuse
But we'll never need a reason for cutting loose
There is no denying the devil in me and you

Never-ending

I saw your cover
And your art drew me in
But the thing about covers
They're only the skin
It's the content inside
That makes a book worthwhile
So I read your blurb
And it made me smile
I grabbed every copy
And cleared off the shelf
For yours is a story
I want for myself
I've read every word
A hundred or more times
Each time I'm grateful
I'm in the plot line
A life changing story
Perpetually revised
Words always added
Updated with time
Bindings may crack
And covers may bend
But your story is magic
For it never ends

Our Forever

When did you know
That we were meant to be
That your piece of forever
Was wrapped up like me
That your wants and needs
Could be met by this man
That we had been blessed
By Fate and her plan
I can place the moment
That I realized
That my forever love
Was in front of my eyes
It was simple really
It wasn't a trick
It's when our souls aligned
With a magnetic 'click'
Everything made sense
My compass was true
I knew without question
My forever was you

Creature Mine

Darkness, divine
Oh creature of mine
I've waited for you
Across a sea of time
Flesh and bone
Turned to stone
Until the day
You found your way home
Water and fire
We so admire
Our magical powers
Fuel our desire
Push comes to shove
Heaven above
You gave me life
When you gave me
your love

Destination

My mind is going
In a thousand directions
Around the globe
And back again
But it matters not
Where my thoughts go
For they all wind up
At you

Perfect

The intellect of a goddess
And the body to match
Everything about you
Makes my breath catch
The sound of your voice
Or touch of your hand
That look in your eye
Each curly strand
The curl of your smile
Your rapier wit
The glorious booty
On which you sit
Morning time coffee
Afternoon nap
Read 'til sleep takes you
With your head in my lap
There's not a moment
I'll ever regret
Out of all of our lives
This is the best one yet

Sunset

The day begins with fire
Igniting the horizon
A firework launched into the sky
Every morn enlivened
From eye's first open
To sleep's embrace
I feel your touch upon my skin
As the sun lights up your face
I reach out and touch your heart
Hearing the song within your chest
Loving you from day to night
As the sun dances from east to west
In the evening the embers drop
The sun descends below horizon's line
The orange glow its final breath
Caressing our skin one last time
If we have a favorite time
As shadows pay off daytime's debts
It's when the day gives way to night
And we kiss as the sun sets

Time Remains

Every other breath
I breathe for you
Filling your lungs with air
And when you need a safe embrace
I'll breathe you in
And hold you there
Every other heartbeat
I give to you
Pushing blood
Through your veins
And when you need a place to rest
I'll squeeze you into my heart
And keep you as long as time remains
As for heartbeats and breaths
I must hold some in reserve
So when I get your call
Saying you need the rest of me
I will have more to give
And you can have it all

Roam

I can devour you with my eyes
Filled with need and want
You see my desire plain
My ache bordering on pain
The most pleasurable taunt
I can devour you with my mouth
My lips upon your skin
Hips thrash and rise
While I'm between your thighs
Wallowing in sin
I can devour you with my mind
As your hands begin to roam
Your thoughts under my control
Our bodies together and whole
In each other we've found our home

Harvest

Late at night you call to me
In your thoughts and in your dreams
My mind, alert, hears your plea
For you've consumed all of me
Mind, body, and soul, it seems
You've ate me up and set me free
You're my lock and I'm your key
We work together as a team
A better fit there cannot be
You're the flower to my bee
Giving nectar in honeyed streams
Letting me harvest it with glee
A better fate I'll never see
Than being part of Fate's scheme
We as two as one, eternally

Caregiver

I wrap my arms around you
And hold you so very tight
Making sure you're safe and warm
And sleeping through the long dark night
When we wake upon the morn
Sun breaks the edge of dawn
I'll hold on a while more
My guarding wolf to your fawn
As the day proceeds apace
The night begins to loom once more
I am drawn right back to you
The raging surf upon your shore
You take my hand and pull me near
Wolf and fawn are changing place
I retreat into your arms
Where you'll keep me warm and safe

Haunted

The ghosts of things left unsaid
Drag their fingers up my spine
So I've vowed to always tell you
All the varied thoughts of mine
Every way in which you move me
Effects you see and some you can't
The ways you make me a better man
Or how one look puts me in a trance
How you make me taut with need
My body coiled like a spring
Or the way that just for you
My healed heart will always sing
There's a million things I love about you
A million ways to make you mine
A million ways to give you myself
And you'll see them all in time

Inferno

I have a fire
Deep inside
It's always burning
This desire of mine
I'm like a rocket
Blasting through the sky
Or a viper ready to strike
Once you've caught my eye
Every thought of you
Makes me vibrate with need
Two wolves on the hunt
Moving at speed
Ever my equal
In all that we do
This truth is eternal
I burn for you

Known

I knew your touch
Before your fingers graced my skin
I knew your soul
Before you released the glow within
I knew your song
Before I ever heard your voice
I knew your bliss
Before we had cause to rejoice
I knew your beauty
Before I was able to see
I knew your heart
Before you gave it to me
I knew your love
Before I knew it was you
It took one fated moment
To make it all come true

In You

In you I find
Elegance
In your movements
Melody
In your voice
Empathy
In your actions
Passion
In your choice
Wisdom
In your words
Love
In your heart
Magick
In your eyes
That claimed me
From the start

Unburden

The binding thread sings to me tonight
Head lolled back like I've taken a punch
And maybe I have
With every ounce of pain you feel
Being this connected
Feeling your pain
Is a million times better
Than feeling nothing
And I'm honored if
For even one moment
I help carry that weight
So you don't have to
Bear it alone

Visionary

The look in your eyes
Beckons
When we touch and the electricity
Crackles
And every cell in my body
Demands
That we we give in to our
Desire
And become what we've been
Destined
To become from the
Beginning
And claim our rightful
Power
Which Fate has upon us
Bestowed
And I can see it all when I
Look
Into your eyes

Lupine

No amount of forever
Is going to count
As high as I want it to
For me to spend with you
Every sunrise from now
Until the sun dies
Will be too few
For me to spend with you
Eternal afternoon delights
Where you make me swoon
With your eyes so blue
Are insufficient to spend with you
Each full moon
With lupine pull
Harvest, blood or blue
Aren't enough to spend with you
Morning, noon, and night
Endings are too soon
There's just one thing to do
And that's spend them all with you

Never Enough

Enough of you
Is anathema to my very existence
It's like saying I've breathed enough
Or my heart has beat enough
I will never get enough heartbeats
Enough breaths
Or enough time with you

Carried Home

I carry you in each heart beat
And hold you in each breath
You live in every waking thought
And every dream while I rest
I'm infused with you completely
My flesh my blood my bone
As long as there is life in me
You'll always have a home

When I'm Lost

You're my anchor
On a tempest-tossed sea
A jailbreak
When I need set free
A signal fire
When I'm lost and need found
The voice in my ear
When no one else is around
You keep me safe
And help me get home
You live in my dreams
So I'm never alone
The source of my smile
And cause of my laugh
My guiding compass
To show the right path
All that I am
And all that I do
Since Fate introduced us
Is colored by you

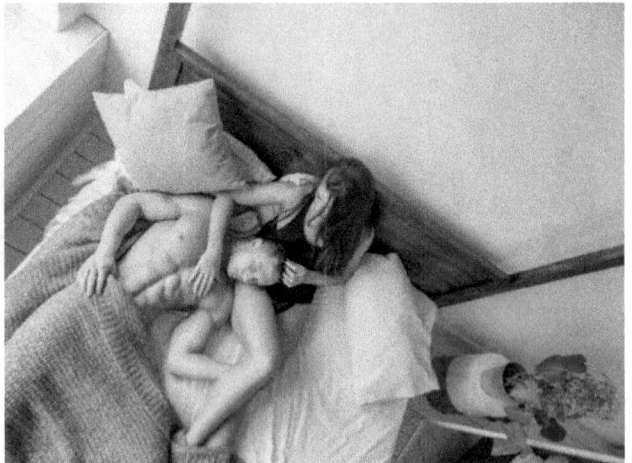

HA Blackwood

Moonlight Pursuit

Your moonlight draws me out to sea
A siren song I just adore
Crossing over the midnight cusp
I turn and chase you back to shore
I find myself in the woods
Your slivers dancing though the boughs
Though the woods are cold and dark
I feel warm and safe somehow
You dance upon the snowy fields
Making daytime from the night
Silver and blue your magic tints
Infused within galactic light
I gaze upon you in the sky
Your gravity pulls me close
Your arm are waiting open wide
To hold me where I'm needed most

Winter Storm

Every snowflake is unique
In its shape and design
So it is with thoughts of you
And the way you make me rhyme
Every thought a piece of you
Each one uniquely refined
They pile up like flakes of snow
Drifting deep inside my mind
I close my eyes and see them all
As if by magick they start to swarm
Assembled in the perfect way
An image of you starts to form
I see your eyes in color blue
The soft curves of your lovely face
I catch a glimpse of a fantasy
A vision of beauty wrapped in lace
I hear a voice that makes me swoon
Kissing with words only I can hear
A heart that makes my flower bloom
A soul that makes my own appear
Millions, billions, trillions of thoughts
Inside my mind forever accrue
I find that I am gladly buried
In a never-ending blizzard of you

If You're Lucky

If you're lucky
There will be moments
Where there's you before
And you after
Truths revealed
Eyes wide
Mind open
If you're lucky
You'll see these moments
As they happen
Feel them as they come
I heard it when
Our magnets clicked
Felt it when
The thread pulled tight
Mind wide
Heart open
We were lucky
I was done
And we began

A Certain Effect

They flitter and flutter their way around
One of nature's most beautiful sights
Paper thin and delicate
Yet somehow they take flight
In the right situation
They bring me to my knees
And the amazing thing about them
Is that they do it with such ease
It happens when I lay my eyes on you
And the emotions that it brings
It's true that the world can change
By the flapping of a butterflies wings

Hues

Blue
Sky
As far as your
Eyes
Can see
As deep as the
Ocean
Can be
Where the light turns
Purple
Like the
Sunset
At the end of the day
Like your
Soul
When it comes out to play
Every color I see
So vibrant and true
Are tinted by your magic
Which starts deep inside
Your eyes of blue

Light And Magick

All the letters
Arranged in all the words
In all the languages
Known to humanity
Will never be enough
To adequately describe
How I feel about you
But I'll keep writing
Until they do
Because you're made of grace
And light and magick
And you're worth it

Fantasy

I have dreams and fantasies
Involving me and you
Places that we'll go and
Things that we will do
Relaxing in a cabin
Or lounging by the sea
It doesn't matter what it is
As long as it's you and me
We could take a rocket ride to mars
Or fight a zombie horde
Regardless what we decide to do
We won't ever get bored
We could make a sexy movie
We could make the sequel too
As long as we're together, love
My fantasy's come true

Multiple Choice

Life presents unlimited choices
That spawn infinite universes
In one, I made that light
In another, I made that phone call
In this one, I sent that message
Each choice has an outcome
Every outcome a consequence
But no matter the choice
And what the result
In this universe
And all of the others
The destination is the same
It's always been you

Descriptive

How do I describe
What your love feels like
Without describing what sunshine
Feels like on your skin
Or the smell of fresh rain
The way a thunderclap
Vibrates in your chest
What a smile feels like
Or how butterflies
Make my stomach flip
Some feelings
You have to experience
For yourself
But if I had to find
A single word to describe
What your love feels like
I'd say
It feels like home

Ethereal Vapors

Nights are lonely for some
But I've not found them to be
For whenever I wake up
You're right next to me
When I close my eyes
And go back to sleep
We're off and running
New adventures we seek
We'll ride on a cloud
Down a rainbow road
At the end of which
Is our pot of gold
Ethereal vapors
We travel the world
My eyes on fire
Like your radiant curls
We swim 'cross the sea
And soar through the air
Lead the way, baby
I'll follow you there

Scry

I find you
In the starry sky above
Lighting up every night
Seen by every ageless wight
Sending messages of love
I find you
In the deep of the blue sea
Married to the moon
Cleansing ancient wounds
Saving our souls by decree
I find you
Up on mountain high
Where the air is rare and thin
I hear your voice upon the wind
Whispering the things you scry
I find you
In everything I see
Passion, wisdom, and beauty too
All I am is claimed by you
And never have I felt so free

Cupid's Arrow

I crept along on silent feet
Earth and foot did scarcely meet
Not a sound did I make
I saw your tracks upon the ground
My heart picked up its steady pace
My ears tuned in to any sound
I sniffed the wind to catch your scent
Your pheromones an intoxicant
I knew that you were somewhere near
That we were getting danger close
But I had no cause to fear
The very thing I wanted most
A whisper slicing through the air
I barely knew that it was there
I never felt the arrow part
Front to back, through and through
For the hole inside my heart
Was destined to be filled by you

Lock and Key

In the pitch black of night
The world is quiet
But my mind is loud
A thousand things running
Alone, my own crowd
I try to focus on one thing
To put things in order
To make words come out
There's so much noise
My mind is locked down
It's actually quite simple
To make these words flow
I know just what to do
The key to my poems
I just think of you

This Love

I felt it the moment that we met
I just didn't realize it yet
It was always a certain bet
That we would fall in love
I see in you the magick moon
O'er the earth your light is strewn
From my chest my heart is hewn
To give to you my love
In all our lives that came before
From mountain high to oceans shore
We had it all and wanted more
A forever kind of love
We walked a path set by Fate
She always knew the time and date
And oh my god you were with the wait
To share with you this love

Under The Moon

Our nights are a series of moments
Be they great or small
It matters not, I want them all
For they each contain a piece of you
Like in the dark unsettled night
When I wake and see your face
Before you vanish without a trace
I wonder if you think of me too
I know the answer is a happy yes
With a sated smile and pleasant sigh
I hold you close and close my eyes
And let the darkness collect its due
The curves of our bodies mold to fit
As we make the most of the night
We chase our dreams ahead of the light
And the morning which comes too soon
We pass the day with tasks at hand
Counting the minutes until the dusk
Happy in love and drunk with lust
When again we can frolic under the moon

In Between

My favorite
moments
Are often unseen
Interstitial vignettes
Those times in between
The moment after
A passionate kiss
Or the realization
Of a feeling like this
It's the moment I see you
In the morning light
The touch of your lips
When we kiss goodnight
The way that you linger
When I wake from a dream
Or the knowledge you're always
A part of my team
These tiny moments
Loom large in my view
For each of them serve
As a reminder of you

Artisan

If I were a rockstar
I'd write for you a hit
The music and the lyrics
Always seem to fit
If I were a painter
You're my masterpiece
Your colors and your beauty
Never seem to cease
If I were a sculptor
Forming stone and steel
I would carve your likeness
So you can see just what I feel
Instead I am a writer
Words are my milieu
So I'll put pen to paper
To pay homage to you

What If

If I knew then what I know now
Would I do things the same
It's an interesting question
This what-if game
If I knew I would end up
In exactly the same place
Would I make earlier moves
Speed up the chase
But that's not how it works
When you change your impulse
You make different choices
You get different results
The universe unfolds
Exactly as it should
I wouldn't want to change that
Even if I could
So I'd walk the same path
Time after time
Trusting that Fate
Will always make you mine

Lyrical Miracle

There are lyrics
In hundreds of songs
The authors didn't know us
But they're not wrong
Prince didn't know
That nothing compares to you
But that doesn't mean
That the statement's untrue
When Zeppelin wrote Thank You
And said inspiration is what you are
They couldn't know that
You'd be my guiding star
Ed Sheeran said you look perfect
And there's no way he realized
He was singing about you
When seen through my eyes
And the thousand years
Of which Christina Perri sang
Wasn't about us
But how true it rang
There are so many songs
With lyrics so smart
That remind me of you
And your place in my heart

Balance

The moon has her sun
Each other they adore
Perfectly matched
Like the sea and her shore
Thunder goes with lightning
The flash that brings the peal
One a treat for the eyes
The other you can feel
Flowers need the bee
To make them bloom
And bees need the flower
To fill their honeycomb
The wolf is incomplete
In a world without his mate
Nature craves that balance
So we were matched by Fate

Heart to Heart

Some words I write the world will see
Others are meant for you and me
Some are written off the cuff
While yours are born within my heart
Some are written just for fun
Others have meaning I wish to impart
I have thoughts I'll never share
Except to you my soul I'll bare
You have a knack to understand
The things that run through my head
You gently take me by the hand
And hold me 'til my soul's been bled
Each day's first words are yours alone
And you always give them a home
I know you as well as you know me
So my words will find their mark
And it's very plain to see
The home you make is in your heart

Time After Time

Traveling through space
And tripping through time
We hit on the path
Where Fate made you mine
It wasn't dumb luck
Or pure happenstance
'Twas meant to be
It wasn't just chance
When you've lived and loved
As much as we have
You know the feeling
When you're on the right path
A thousand lives before
We've met just like this
Seemingly random events
Impossible to resist
Magnetic forces draw us
No matter how far
I am your planet
You are my star
Time after time
We don't keep score
As much as you're mine
I'm forever yours

Carry On

Wings spread wide
You carry me
When I cannot go on
With an understanding
Only you can have
You give me your strength
Lift me up
And help me put one foot
Ahead of the other
So that I may open my wings
And carry you
When the time comes

Flash and Sizzle

You're all thunder and lightning
I'm rainfall and petrichor
Two halves of the whole
Leave us wanting more
More of the thunder
More of the rain
All of the pleasure
None of the pain
I'm the cover of a book
You've always wanted to read
You are the story
On the pages between
An interesting cover
Makes you want to open the book
But it's the content that turns the pages
Not how the volume looks
You're the flash and the sizzle
The content and the plot
You bring the cleansing rain
And keep the story hot
You complete the puzzle
The half that makes me whole
The mind and body may change
But you always have my soul

Hand In Hand

We stumble into darkness
Time and time again
Hands reaching, searching
Yearning to touch our skin
We rumble with our demons
And battle to the end
Back to back and hand in hand
Our will will never bend
We tumble into each other
Heads going over heels
Hearts emerging from the dark
And showing our love is real

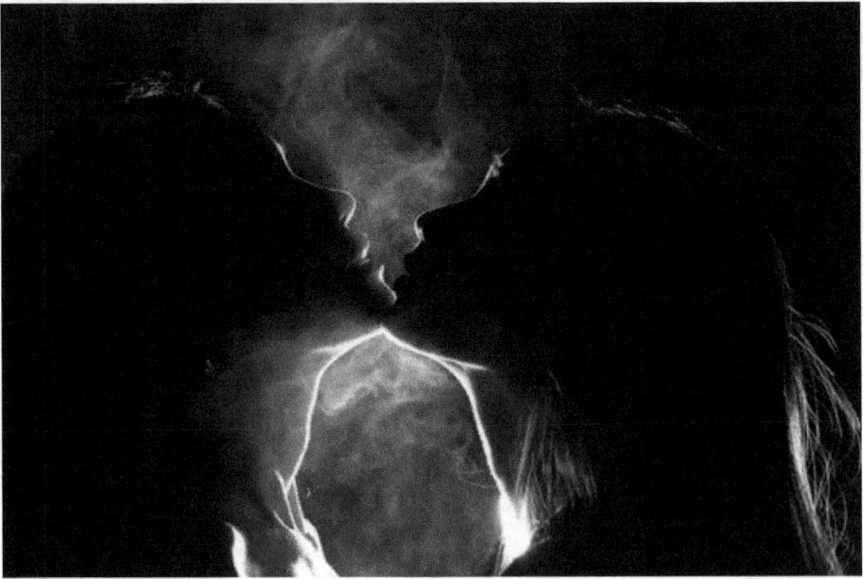

Edge of a Dream

There's danger in the air
Creatures everywhere
Ready to attack
We're more than up to task
We never have to ask
We have each other's back
Around the world we sneak
Using all of our mystique
The darkness stabs at us
As sharp as any knife
A risk to limb and life
But we have each other's trust
There's a place I want to go
That only you and I know
For the entrance to be seen
The angle must be just right
For it's hidden out of sight
Waiting on the edge of a dream

Objets D'arts

I've said it before
You are the artist
And also the art
Your beauty is timeless
And was from the start
Our roles are defined
In this play of ours
We each play our part
There's no better team
Than when we compart
I'm yours evermore
'Til the end of the 'verse
These words I impart
Your home is forever
Inside my heart

Bones

My bones were made
From the ash of a thousand lives
So they would remember
The way you felt
And find their way back to you
Upon my bones
Was carved your name
So they would know you
When we met
And open their secrets to you
My heart was taught
A language known only to you
So when you spoke, it would know
You had come for your claim
And at long last
We were home

Weatherman

Of all the times the sun's come up
And shined upon the earth
Of all the days that rain came down
And washed away the dirt
All the times the wind did blow
Rattling foundations of stone
And all the times the snow piled up
Trying to keep us home
Never did the springtime rains
Ruin our happy mood
The sound of raindrops coming down
Always makes us feel good
When winter gales block the roads
It's never cause for despair
We simply light a roaring fire
And enjoy the crackling air
Of all the times the sun's come up
And shined upon the land
It's never felt as good to me
As when you hold my hand

Enticed

Like the snake to his charmer
The moth to a flame
I'm helplessly drawn
To the sound of your name
The galaxies in your eyes
Have a gravity of their own
When you fix your gaze upon me
Their pull brings me home
Those lips are like heaven
The cannot be real
But if I love my life just right
I'll find out how they feel
Like honey to the bear
The flower to the bee
Everything about you
Is so enticing to me

Maestro

You can play me like a fiddle
With your fingers in place of bows
You'll make my body sing your tune
In ways that only you know
I'll conduct you like an orchestra
Your body all in sync
Each piece of you knows its role
In this symphony of kink
When we rehearse our masterpiece
Nothing shall distract us
Going for pleasure, like Carnegie Hall
Takes practice, practice, practice

Sky High

A slip of the lip
The sway in your hips
I'm lost in your sea
Captain of your ship
The shine of your smile
Each passing mile
The passage of time
So worth our while
The look in your eye
A breast-heaving sigh
You are my drug
And you get me so high
A hug and a kiss
Shared moments of bliss
Nothing in the world
Can be better than this

Timeless

From the dawn of time
Until the sands run out
I have loved your soul
There can be no doubt
From runes etched in stone
Until the ink runs dry
I've written about you
And the things you scry
I've told the world
Time and again
Of your loving heart
And your delicate skin
Of your warrior's spirit
And magick eyes
Of your powerful wings
When you take to the skies
Every word you speak
Is a love letter to my heart
Each moment together flies
Eternity each second apart
From the earth's roaring seas
To its glistening shores
In each life we've lived
My soul has been yours

Addicted

You're the book I can't put down
Until I consume each word
The TV show I have to binge
Until the last line is heard
You're the game I have to play
Until the final boss is beat
I'll play your every level
And never try to cheat
Some would say I'm addicted
And it's kind of hard to refute
Once I got a taste of you
My desire was absolute
No matter the analogy
The common thread is true
We will live a thousand lives
And I'll never get enough of you

Because There's You

The roughest day
Holds no sway
Over what I do
Or what I say
Because there's you
When I scream and shout
In any amount
Overcome with joy
There can be no doubt
Because there's you
When I feel inspired
And my neurons have fired
I accomplish great things
And feel admired
Because there's you
All that I've done
The battles I've won
It all means so much
And it's all just begun
Here with you

Born Anew

I never thought my name was beautiful
Until it passed your lips
The resonance brought me to my knees
Like everything I'd heard before
Was simple background noise
I never thought my skin special
Until I felt your fingertips
The electricity that passed from you to me
Like a circuit completed
Born anew under your touch
I never thought my heart unique
Until it was within your grip
Each beat now alive with song
My chambers fit inside your fists
Meant for you all along

Storied

You set me on fire
But I never burn
The heat in my veins
Is of no concern
I fell for your flames
And seek their return
I take your words
With a stroke of the pen
Touching your mind
Igniting, and then
Leaving you breathless
Again and again
Made for each other
In every way
We fell together
Our love on display
A storied romance
As written by Fate

Like

I love you like fire
You love me like rain
Opposite forms of magic
Yet they feel the same
You make me weak
In a very good way
Yet I feel stronger
With each passing day
You steal my breath
And my heart beats so fast
Our love together
Was made to last
You glow like the moon
And shine like the sun
I'm drawn like your tides
And sure you're the one

Playmates

A rip in the sky
Our souls sailing by
Waiting for us to dive in
We make for the hole
Soul chasing soul
So the game of love can begin
It's always the same
The point of this game
To find where the joy lies within
We play with such pride
We're on the same side
For this game we both get to win

Animalistic

A tourmaline sky
And fields of jade
Under a topaz moon
Our future is made
No one can see us
We shift in the night
Cunning and swift
With superior sight
Faster than lightning
As slippery as rain
Naked and fearless
We feel no shame
Moving in tandem
On two legs or four
As much as I get of you
I'll always want more
Stronger together
We'll always be
We run 'til we're sated
Wild and free

Pursuit

Scent on the wind
Nostrils flare
Hunger grows
I know you're there
Instinct takes command
I must hunt you
And make you mine
The ground shakes
Vibrations resonate
To the bone
The chase can't wait
You lead me deep
Into the place
You know best
Where I'll catch you
Only because
You want to be caught
And make me yours

Moonlight

Fresh layer of snow
Full moon's glow
Changing the landscape
For those down below
Shadows they grow
The beasts start to roam
The deep of the night
Is calling us home
Shedding our skin
Nose to the wind
Hunter and hunted
The game can begin
On the prowl
An exchange of growls
The battle is swift
A victory howl
Come the sun's rise
That look in your eyes
Wrapped in your arms
We each claim our prize

Passage Of Time

Voices lost to time
Ages go by
Still here together
Are you and I
Lines change on a map
Empires rise and fall
Power is ever fleeting
Yet we have seen it all
Flood waters ebb
Glaciers will melt
We've played all the hands
That we have been dealt
We watched the big bang
And stars go super nova
And each life with you
I'd live over and over

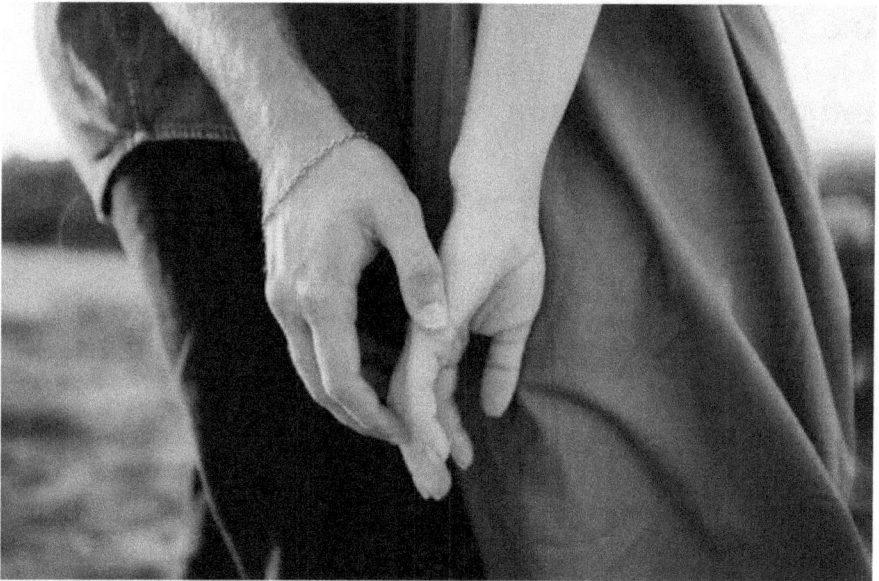

Among The Stars

When I close my eyes
I am at your side
Your hand in mine
My shooting star
When I close my eyes
I can hear your heart sing
The melody the most beautiful thing
A symphony without end
When I close my eyes
I can taste your lips
Full moon's eclipse
Electric sugar on my tongue
When I close my eyes
Mother of pearl
And ebony swirled
Shadows of love and light
I look in your eyes
And I'm yours, I find
What's more, you're mine
And we go dancing among the stars

Destiny

We stand together at the edge of all
Bodies close, fingers laced
Looking through time like a window
At everything that's taken place
All the different paths we've walked
And the places to which they've led
All the laughs and husky moans
The triumphs felt and tears we shed
Every story comes to an end
As we watch the next begin
The memories are crisp and sharp
With you and I contained within
Eons pass before our eyes
Stretching off through time and space
An eternity of lives and loves
And being lost within your gaze
We turn and face the future now
The swirling mist both dark and light
You give my hand an extra squeeze
Our destiny is ours to write

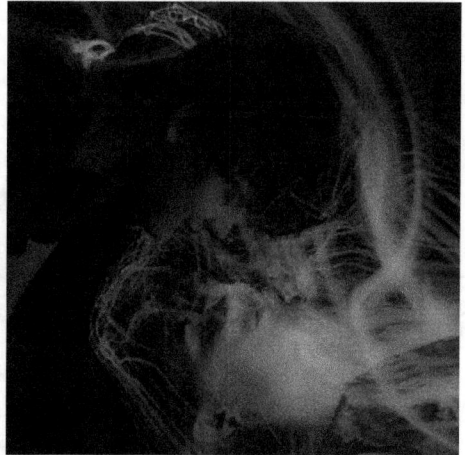

Complete

I thought I knew love
It turns out I was wrong
It's not just a feeling
Or a dedicated song
It's a part of your being
Infused in your soul
It's knowing you've got me
Where ever I go
It's how each thought
Is blessed by your touch
How as much as I can get
Is never too much
It's that feeling I get
In the dead of the night
And I have to reach out
To make sure you're alright
It's the way that you knock me
Right on my seat
But mostly it's that feeling
That you make me complete

Vistas Of Time

I've sailed across every ocean
Seen the dark side of the moon
Nothing out there could prepare me
For the way you make me swoon
I've crawled through briar and thorn
Walked on the surface of the sun
I've never felt anything as intensely
As the way that I feel your love
I've fought through armies of demons
Slayed every dragon I could find
Not even death could prevent me
From finding you and making you mine
I've never really wanted a kingdom
I never had a desire to rule
When sweeping over vistas of time
I only felt the magick of your pull
Across the generations you called me
Like you've done a thousand times before
We followed our path until the magnets clicked
And you grabbed me and made me yours

Resonance Divine

I wish you knew what it felt like
Each time I see your face
The racing pulse
The stolen breath
The mental embrace
I wish you could see yourself
The way my eyes show
Your soul alight
Brilliance on display
Oh, then you'd know
I wish you could hear
The melody of your voice
A symphony of one
Resonance divine
Leaving no choice
Wishes can come true
We've been given the gift of time
Each day I can find another way
To show you your magick
And just why I made you mine

Not Today

There may come a day
When I don't know what to say
When my words won't flow
And my ink runs dry
But not today
There may come a time
When the stars won't shine
And the moon won't glow
Under a blackening sky
But not today
We may find a place
Where there's not a trace
Of the things that we know
On which we rely
But not today
Today
My words will rhyme
The stars will shine
The moon will glow
On all we know
And surcease our sorrow
If you doubt this simple truth
Read this poem again tomorrow

Homage

If I were an action hero
I'd take a bullet for you
If I were a baseball star
I'd hit a homer or two
If I raced cars
I'd set the record pace
So I'd get home faster
To kiss on that face
But I am a wordsmith
Making language my game
The equipment is different
But the goal is the same
No matter the poem
Or what the words do
I always craft them
To pay homage to you

Ecstasy

You make darkness beautiful
You release the beast within
You make danger sexy
And craft virtue from our sin
My bones ache when we're apart
My soul cries out for your return
Pain and pleasure intertwined
The hotter the flame the sweeter the burn
Bedroom, glen, or forest deep
Our primal nature needs to run
Gripping flesh and gnashing teeth
Gasping breaths and heartbeats drum
Moonlight glows where bodies lie
Ecstasy wrapped and soaking wet
Fully used from tip to tail
Frenzied need a clock reset
You make darkness beautiful
You can tame the beast within
Feral still but forever yours
And always ready to shed my skin

Fuss

One day you'll see
Yourself the way I do
You'll feel the hitch
In your breath
The rush of heat
To your skin
The way your pulse pounds
In your chest
The way you were whole
But incomplete
Until Fate brought us together
One day you'll see
Yourself the way I do
And you'll understand
What the fuss is all about

Giving Back

When I'm running on empty
You fill me up
When I'm stranded on base
You bat cleanup
No matter the issue
Or struggle I face
You've got my back
And put trouble in it's place
When I'm drowning in sin
And covered in shame
You wash me clean
Baptized by your name
It may have been fated
Just a matter of course
But you saved my soul
When you claimed me as yours
As much as you give
And as much as you do
I'll spend my life
Giving back to you

Asleep

I wake in the night
Demon's wings beating
The air
Was I dreaming
Or is it really
Out there
Nightmare fading
I reach 'cross the dark
For you
I wonder if
You're reaching for
Me too
I hold you close
And wrap you in
My arms
No demon's dream
Will ever do
You harm
Heavenly, my name
From your lips
Does seep
And with your love
You lull me back
Asleep

Second Sight

You hung upon a crescent moon
Dangling far above the sea
Watching with your sapphire eyes
What will become of you and me
Dancing in an autumn wood
Casting spells with magick pure
Heaven sent and lilac bloom
Balance brought and future sure
Always like does call to like
And so with us on down the line
From start of all to final end
Our souls connect and bodies bind
Second sight in immortal realm
On each other we do rely
Instinct driven and purpose bound
A certain path you can espy
You hung upon a crescent moon
Daring the world to knock you down
Laughing because you always knew
I'd never let you hit the ground

Kindling

I am kindling for your spark
Just a moment is all it took
And I burst into passion's flame
From a word, an image, or a look
Burning desire is the fuel
Which keeps this fire ever bright
All I need to add is you
And I'm burning through the night
The thing I love about this blaze
The fire burning on repeat
You know exactly what you do
And you gleefully bring the heat
What makes me smile even more
As if I ever have a choice
Is that your fire burns like mine
From a look, a touch, or just my voice
The two of us are set aflame
And have been since the day we met
We gave the stars their burning glow
The universe is in our debt

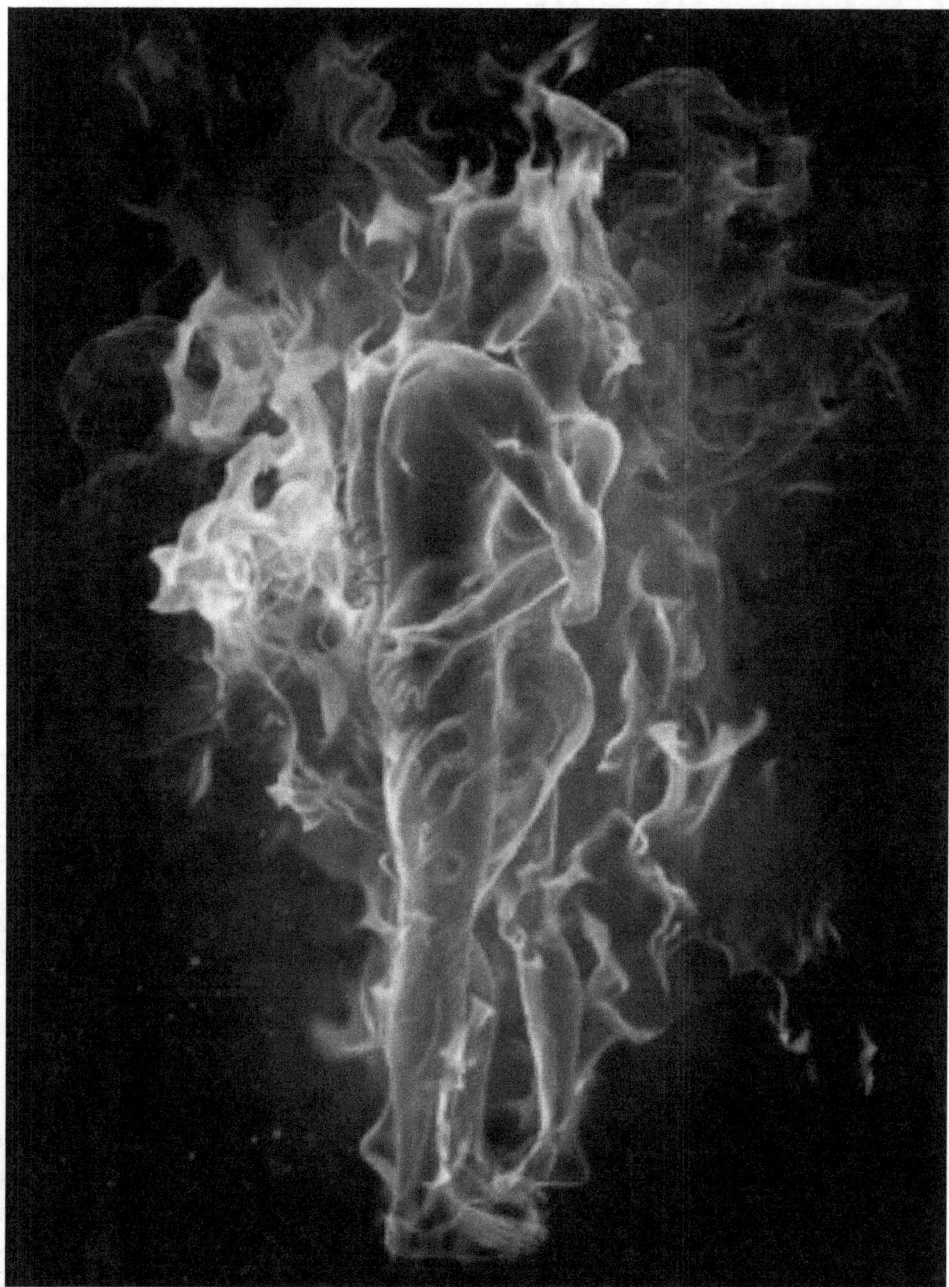

Walking The Line

Lips like sugar
Sweet upon my tongue
Skin as soft as butter
Slides beneath my thumb
Your body is a new land
Freshly explored each time
Teasing out your secrets
As I make you mine
Everything about you
Designed to lure me in
Predator or prey
The line between is thin
It doesn't really matter
On which side that coin will fall
In this magic world of ours
We get to have it all

Electric

Every gift you make to me
I'm happy to receive
And once you let me in your world
I knew I'd never leave
Every thing I long to be
I see within your eyes
Your friend, your lover, your fated mate
Your devil in disguise
I feel you in the midnight rain
Electric air and petrichor
Breathe you deep and take you in
Touch my skin and make me yours
Never in the course of time
Will come another love like ours
Played out over a million lives
Felt in the heart but born in the stars

Glows

I'd know you no matter where we go
I'll always remember how your soul glows
It's so beautiful
In another life far from here
I'll still see you crystal clear
You're unforgettable
We're time travelers, life by life
Our love grows stronger every time
It's unstoppable
I change my shape and bare my teeth
You change yours too, to my relief
We're atypical
You take my hand and lead me home
And never more shall we be alone
We're inseparable
Fate ensures we always meet
Whole apart, together complete
We're inevitable

Affected

Of all the ways you affect me
It's hard to pick my fave
You steal my breath
And my heart pounds
Every time I see your face
You have a brilliant mind
And you show it off quite well
You challenge me
To keep your pace
My brain using every cell
I have dreams about you
Some adventurous and benign
Others drip
With wanton need
In which I make you mine
No matter how you slice it
There's an answer here I find
In the end it's obvious
The best way you affect me
Is that you're always on my mind

Encore

Soft music plays
And I close my eyes
Visualizing the notes
And just where they lie
Upon your body
Each note a kiss
I'll play you an opus
While bringing you bliss
Piano and woodwinds
Percussion and strings
I'll master them all
Your body will sing
When the concert is over
And you're longing for more
You can rest assured
I'll play an encore

Some Days

Life can intrude
On a perfect day
No schedule
No warning
It's really quite rude
There's nothing to be done
On a day such as this
You can't fight the current
You just roll with the punches
Once the day has
begun
But one thing is true
We're never alone
No matter what
I've got your back
And you got mine too

Pages

Dragging pen over parchment is akin
To sliding my tongue across your skin
Every movement purpose serves
To stimulate your vital nerves
Every word that does alight
Upon your flesh or paper white
Leaves a mark forever burned
Goosebumps raised and pages turned
I'll save my place with a special mark
That keeps the pages spread apart
Writing a story I want to read
Creating a world that drips with need
A better story cannot be told
Than the one that is written where your pages fold
The title etched along the spine
Leaves no doubt the story is mine

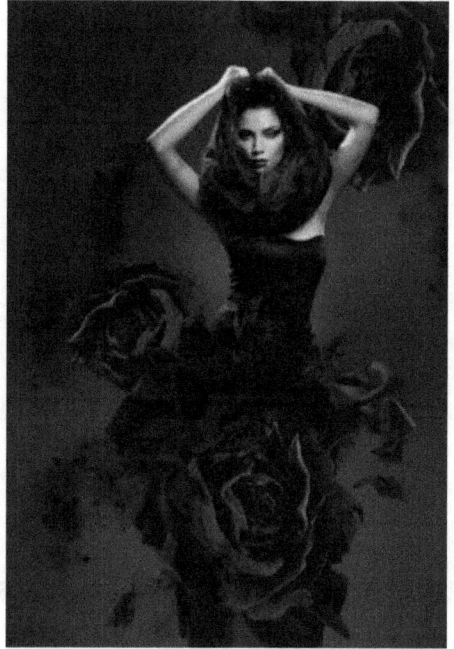

Petals

Hope springs eternal
So the saying goes
Every time I see you
You're like a fresh spring rose
The sun bends its will
To shine on you its light
Your colors bursting forth
Showing off your might
Your bud is just as beautiful
As when you show your bloom
Your thorns may help protect you
But your petals make me swoon
Through the long cold winter
Your roots grew deep and strong
It's the same with this love of ours
And we knew it all along

Drugged

I wish that I could bottle
The way you make me feel
I could take it out and use it
When I need a little zeal
My mind feels electric
And my heart beats like a drum
My breath flows at a rapid pace
And my body starts to hum
These effects are autonomic
And happen with no control
It's because you are my fated mate
We're connected soul to soul
There is no drug prescribed
Or on the black market found
That will ever have the same effect
As you do when you're around
It happened the first time we spoke
The first time you said my name
And every day from then to now
I've never been the same
If I could bottle that feeling
I don't think that I would
Because it's being next to you
That makes me feel so good

Forecast

Westerly winds blow
Driving rain and snow
Flashes of lightning
As the storm starts to roll
Seas can roll and boil
Tornadoes twist and turn
Temperatures can soar
And wildfires burn
Hurricanes and mudslides
Disasters, not the drinks
We will always out last them
For they give us time to think
Hatches battened down
To keep us safe and warm
With you at my side
We can weather any storm

Inside

There was a time long ago
The world knew not your name
Your deeds and work they knew quite well
But you had no use of fame
You made the sky as blue as your eyes
And rose with the sun in the east
In fields of green your artwork is seen
Along with the white toothed beasts
Wherever you go you leave your mark
Your beauty has colored the plains
Wildflowers grow where your feet touch the ground
And you light up the sunset in flames
I knew you then as I know you know
Our souls they never shall part
The most beautiful thing you've ever done
Is take me inside of your heart

Searching

I swam across the ocean
But you weren't upon the beach
I ran across the continent
But you were always out of reach
I climbed the highest mountain
It took me halfway to the moon
From this towering vantage point
I sang your favorite tune
My voice carried world wide
But I never saw your face
So I searched in every nation
And I looked for you in space
When I need to find you, love
There's nothing I won't do
Nothing in the universe
Can keep me away from you
When I finally found you
You were standing at my side
A smile wide across your face
Like you were busting out with pride
You said you knew I'd find you
That I would go to any length
That you were with me all along
And that's where I got my strength
We're together all the time, you said
No matter where we go
We carry each other in our hearts
And are wrapped within our souls

About The Author

Hi! I'm HA Blackwood. It's a pen name, but I've grown pretty fond of it. I love the people I've met undertaking this adventure in writing erotic romance. I've made a lot of friends and we've had a lot of fun together. Don't read too much into that. Wink. I love the arid high plains desert of Colorado and enjoy exploring with the boss of me, a feisty beagle with a nose for rabbits and an insatiable love of the trail. There are more adventures planned in my little universe, some with Darcy and Gemma and some with other characters. And there are several more volumes of poems planned so if you enjoy what I've written so far, stick around—you'll be (hopefully) pleasantly surprised.

Other Books From H.A. Blackwood

Tell-Tale Hearts
by H.A. Blackwood

Darcy Ford is coming off an ill-advised relationship that ended in disaster. When she's at her lowest point, she meets a woman who takes her back ten years to a night of wild passion. A night when she met-and lost-someone who opened new worlds to her. A night where her heart was stolen. A night which was the beginning of this most recent disastrous affair. Only by re-telling these tales can she find her way back to her lost love and the return of her heart.

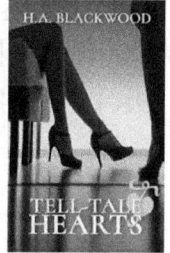

Candid Camera
by H.A. Blackwood

A new relationship. A secret from the past. Will their love survive?

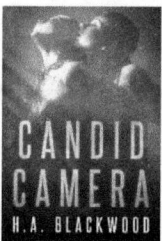

Darcy Ford and Gemma Amante are contemplating the next big move in their relationship when Ashleigh, a lover from Gemma's past, shows up unexpectedly. She brings news that has Darcy and Gemma on a trip to Los Angeles.

Gemma's friends from her old life as a sex worker are in trouble and need help. Going undercover as sex cam workers in the city of sin may seem like a literal pleasure trip, but when they go up against a new type of criminal, they're going to need all of their sexy savvy. Between steamy escapades, clues begin to emerge. If they're going to solve this mystery, they'll have to risk their way of life, their relationship, and their very lives.

Adored (Volume I)
by H.A. Blackwood

Whimsical. Fantastical. Celestial

The poems in this book reflect a lot of different things, but they all have one thing in common: you'll wish they were written about you. You'll wish this was a permanent tribute to you, the reader, on display for the world to see.

Such is the magic of the written word. It can bring out many emotions, but the one you'll be left with after reading this book is simply this: adored.

Other Books From Baying Hound Media

Still Yours
By Cara Roman

High school sweethearts, Ridge left Leigha shortly after graduation to follow his dreams of a career in the music business. Finding his success, but missing home, he is back 12 years later trying to earn a second chance with Leigha. Ridge isn't some 18-year-old teenager anymore, a lot has changed. Can Leigha open up and trust her heart to the man who broke it all those years ago?

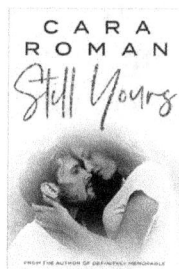

Definitely Memorable
By Cara Roman

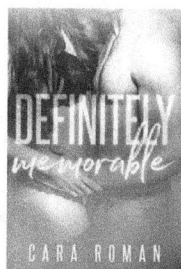

Caitlyn has always dreamed of vacationing in Ireland. After a disappointing divorce she decides its time she does something for herself. What she didn't count on was meeting a charming and devastatingly handsome Irishman, Nolan in a pub. Unable, or unwilling to deny the chemistry between them she throws caution to the wind embarking on a whirlwind romance. Love is never as simple as it seems though, and hers takes a course she never could have predicted.

Without A Wolf (Big Woods Pack Book One)
By Cara Roman

New in town, Emma Lowe was hiding a big secret. Wolf shifter Kian Decker needed to find out who she was, and why she was so very appealing to him. Turns out Emma wasn't the only one in town with secrets. Now their lives have been turned upside down, and they need to figure where they stand.

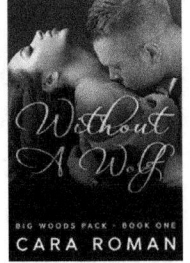

Running From The Wolf (Big Woods Pack Book Two)

The second book in the Big Woods Pack series, Kayla Decker spent years being mad at Lex Kolter. Using her anger as a sheild to keep Lex at bay isn't working so well since the shake ups in the pack. Just when they stop fighting each other new information comes to light threatening the pack once again.